EFFECTIVE MANAGEMENT COACHING

Edwin J Singer is an independent consultant specializing in the problems of people at work. He has worked for public and private organizations, including trade unions. During the last 10 years he has made a special study of the important part coaching can play in management development.

Before starting his own consultancy, E J Singer Associates, he was a senior partner with Urwick, Orr and Partners Ltd, gaining experience in the UK, Europe and North America. He has worked in most industries and many aspects of national and local government. He is a lecturer and writer, a member of the IPM, the Institute of Management Consultants, and a Fellow of the Kingston Regional Management Centre.

He is also author of the IPM book *Training in Industry and Commerce*, revised edition, 1977.

EFFECTIVE MANAGEMENT COACHING

Edwin J Singer

Institute of Personnel Management

DEDICATION

To my wife who is one of the best coaches I know and whose constant encouragement and support helped me to find the time to write this book

First published 1974
Second edition 1979
Reprinted 1981
© *C E J Singer 1974, 1979*

Printed in Great Britain by
Lonsdale Universal Printing Ltd.,
Bath, Avon

ISBN 0 85292 248 5

CONTENTS

FOREWORD

There are many different views on management development but in one area at least there seems to be common agreement; that the majority of individual development takes place on the job and the most significant single developmental factor is the boss-subordinate relationship. One would therefore expect to see considerable emphasis in the management development literature on ways of developing this relationship by effective management coaching. In fact there is relatively little reference material available on the subject, but there is much experience from which to learn. Those who are fortunate will have had the benefit of working under a manager able to correct mistakes in a positive way, to point out implications of proposed action unobserved by the less experienced, to motivate by praise and generally to turn everyday work experience into valued opportunities for personal and professional development.

There are too many who regrettably will not have enjoyed this experience; they will have suffered under managers less gifted in the arts of coaching and counselling their subordinates.

Indeed so important is this aspect of an individual's development that I sincerely believe that the most important consideration in the choice of job for those at the formative stage of their career is the calibre of the person for whom they will work, particularly with regard to the ability to coach.

However, not everyone is a natural coach and even those who are can probably improve their skills by drawing on the experience of others. That is why there has long been a need for a sound guide on the subject, a need now satisfied by Edwin Singer.

He is well qualified to write on the subject of coaching. He has spent most of his working life as a consultant in the training field in which capacity he has had to coach fellow consultants, line managers and personnel managers. Subsequently as a specialist consultant in management development he has had particular experience in coaching in the appraisal situation. Thus he brings a depth of experience over many related fields to his writing.

Coaching is essentially a personal skill. It is therefore necessary to ask whether a book can help to improve one's ability as a coach. I have no doubt that it can—just as books on interviewing have helped countless personnel and line managers to improve their selection skills. But the author would be the first to point out that one learns by doing, and that reading is no substitute for practice. This book explains the essential steps in becoming a skilful coach, after carefully and soundly explaining the need for good coaching and the concepts that underline it. It forms a sound base on which one can practise skills and thereby learn by doing.

All who manage have an obligation to their subordinates to improve their coaching skills. Edwin Singer has provided an excellent text to help us to do this. Those who study it and follow his advice will be bound to make an effective contribution to management development in their companies at the most important level—the day to day working situation.

L D Cowan
Group Personnel Director,
Unigate Ltd,
United Kingdom

PREFACE

Many books have been written about managing and
the techniques of management. There are a number
about management development. Few, however,
have dealt with the means by which knowledge, procedures and thought are translated into practice.
This is not surprising because the means will vary
with each situation. The experienced manager uses
that much maligned word *experience* to help him to
get things done. But what of the new manager, or the
older manager who has been recently promoted? He,
too, is entitled to help and the source of this assistance should be his immediate superior, for he is the
man to show him how to *do* things, to correct his
technique and to add to his knowledge.

This is what coaching is all about. It should be a
work centred activity, which is undertaken as a normal part of any manager's responsibility. The skills
of coaching are best developed by continual practice,
but they can be analysed and understood by those
who recognize their importance. This book attempts
to help those who wish to think more deeply about a
subject which will assist them, as managers, to help
in the development of their subordinates so that they
become yet more effective members of their managerial team. Managers spend a great deal of time considering how to use the financial and material resources
at their disposal. They also give thought to the
deployment of their human resources. They consider
less frequently the need to stimulate their subordinates, throughout the year, so that they wish to

learn, want to explore new avenues, or think how innovation can be purposefully undertaken. This is the life blood of coaching. It is not just another technique of management development; rather it is the process by which the development of managers is achieved through continuous learning in their normal daily environment. To become a successful coach a manager needs to have a genuine concern for the development of others, to be capable of recognizing when a coaching opportunity occurs, and to have learned a sufficient number of the techniques of coaching to be able to apply them well. There are no ready made 'packages' which will enable him to do these things. The starting point must lie in an individual act of determination to coach. Once this has been genuinely undertaken, thinking about what coaching means and making a continual effort to carry out the precepts will lead in time, for that man, to coaching becoming so natural a part of his daily routine that it is no longer a separate technique.

This book is intended to stimulate the reader's thinking rather than to give a prescriptive answer to the question "How do I coach?". Each manager needs to develop a style which will be effective and personal to him. The chapters on job review are included because it is too often thought that an appraisal process alone will lead to an improvement in job performance. Personally I would wish to see the phrase *performance appraisal* dropped from the management literature. Today it carries too many connotations of playing god and is generally disliked by managers and managed alike. *Job review* is a sounder term because it offers the opportunity for reviewing progress, learning lessons and planning action, without the overtone of one man judging another. Management today is increasingly a mutually supportive process in which the manager and his subordinate both learn from each other. For that is how progress is made.

This book is based on countless discussions with colleagues and clients over the years. John Thompson and Ken Myers, briefly with Urwick, Orr and Partners, gave much thought to what coaching really means and I have drawn freely on their thinking. Many other former UOP colleagues have stimulated my thinking, especially John Humble, Nancy Taylor, Keith Lathrope, John Lloyd and Dick Handscombe and Vivian Stokes and various members of the Furniture and Timber Industry Training Board, especially Alan Swaisland. My thanks also to Molins Ltd and Bob Myers for permission to publish the case study in chapter 10.

Finally, my thanks to Nick Cowan for reading the manuscript, making helpful comments and writing the foreword; and to that stalwart believer in the Welsh language, who writes better English than anyone I know, V Hampson-Jones, who has once more edited the writing.

EJS

Preface to second edition

During the five years since the first edition was published the concept of coaching has become more generally accepted in industry and commerce. Fortunately it has not been viewed as just another technique, but rather as an important part of a manager's role which he discharges well or badly in any contact with his subordinates.

My own thinking has also developed during this period and is reflected in the revisions and additions contained in this edition. As usual many people have aided this thought process but special mention is due to Hugh McCredie of the Steetley Company Ltd and Ian Hinton of the Kingston Regional Management Centre.

CHAPTER 1

Why is coaching important?

If it is a manager's job to make the optimum use of the resources at his disposal in order to achieve some defined objective, then everyone in any organization, even the floor sweeper, is a manager. However, common usage restricts the title to those who also have charge of people, although at the bottom of the managerial scale the term is vague. Are supervisors managers and if so what about chargehands? Or is it that managers are not expected to have to work with their hands? There is a level in the managerial scale where decision making has so great an influence on the work of others that we award the job holder the title manager. Managers, therefore, in any organization, have a greater than average responsibility. They are expected to control events, not to be controlled by them. These days they have to take into account changes in technology and markets, and in the environment in which they work.

New ways of helping them to deal with change are the subject of research. Top managers are concerned not only with the development of managers as individuals, but also with the development of the way management, or the managing process, is carried out. To these complexities must be added the gap between what the ordinary citizen expects as his rights in a civil context, and what he finds in reality in the context of organizational life. Combined these can produce organizational disharmony.

If there is to be one social fact which tomorrow's manager must take into account in making his decisions it is that fewer people will be willing to carry out his instructions just because he says so. Think of any organization you like, from Shelter, through industry, to the Civil Service, and ask yourself if managers are not having increasing difficulty in 'managing' the human resource.

Some have tried to meet this problem by improving communications. Tell them the reasons why and then they will accept your decision more readily. I believe that this is an inadequate response to the problem, albeit one in the right direction. It seems to me that our society has reached the stage when citizens wish to control their own destinies to a far greater degree than in the past. Not only have we progressed beyond the stage when a man accepted his station in life, but we have also moved beyond an era when freedom of movement up the social or professional scale was all that was thought necessary for a 'democratic' way of life.

Tomorrow's society will need to acknowledge everyman's right to participate in decision making about matters which directly bear on his daily life. Technology is about to make this possible at a national level. In industry there have been many experiments which demonstrate not only that people can contribute effectively to decision making, but that it is in the organization's interest they should do so. See, for example, the case studies on job enrichment reported by Lynda King Taylor in *Not for Bread Alone*.

Since writing this in the first edition I am able to record an instance of how words can be misunderstood, a subject of great importance referred to in detail in chapters 6 and 7. A managing director of a small company wrote in anger to his trade association complaining that this book advocated a vast increase in the number of committees and that its whole tenor was a reflection of what is wrong with British society. Clearly the gentleman had set patterns in his mind about words like 'participation' and phrases such as 'people can contribute effectively to decision making'.

I have considerable sympathy with this man because words do mean different things to different people. Coaching itself often conjures up the image of teaching a subordinate for a specified time each week in one's office. However, to be effective coaching must be more than 'doing something to someone else' in order that he should develop. Good coaching recognizes that the coach himself will learn; that the subordinate has something to contribute to his boss's thinking; that the process takes place between people, although hopefully one participant has wider and greater experience than the other. A manager who thinks primarily of his hierarchical relationship with his subordinate is unlikely to be effective as a coach. Success will depend primarily on his ability to foster in himself an attitude of mind which is receptive to ideas from his subordinates, one in which he does not think of suggestions as implied criticism; one in which he can discuss freely his own past performance without fear of criticism and without a sense of self-justification. In practice of course all managers coach their subordinates, just as all managers delegate some of their responsibilities. They have to or little would get done. Equally every subordinate is coached by his manager, because over a period he learns what his manager expects of him. The question therefore is not "Should I coach my subordinates?" but rather "How well do I coach them?" And that is what this book is mainly about—developing the skills required to coach effectively. Note the word 'develop'. It is used deliberately, because every manager uses the skills in some way every day of his life. We all listen, discuss, question and summarize. But do we use these skills as well as we should—and are we aware of the impact (or lack of impact) we are making when we use them? In short, when we are coaching our subordinates are we certain that they are learning?

The coaching of individuals by individuals is only one stage in the development of managers and of management development. Let us consider some of the interfaces with other aspects.

To be effective as a coach a manager must earn the respect of his subordinates. That means, quite simply, that he must appear to them to be a good manager. We should focus some attention, then, on a coach's abilities as a manager. Here are a few questions which every manager should at one time or another ask himself:

Do I understand clearly what I am trying to achieve in my job and have I, where possible, attempted to quantify my objectives?

Do I understand clearly how my objectives fit in with the organization's (or unit's) objectives? In other words do I see clearly how my part contributes to the whole?

Do I help to clarify my subordinates' thinking on their own objectives, so that they are able to give positive answers to the first two questions?

Am I capable of focusing attention on the essential matters to achieve my objectives, or do I get bogged down in trivia?

Do I help to focus my subordinates' attention on those things that matter if they are to achieve their objectives?

> When I delegate responsibility do I take the time and
> the trouble to ensure that my subordinate will
> succeed?
>
> Do I and my subordinates have adequate infor-
> mation on which we can monitor our performance
> at each stage so that we can make plans for the
> next phase?
>
> Is this information readily available or is it hidden
> away in a mass of irrelevant information?
>
> Do I recognize that subordinates will expect to be
> rewarded equitably?
>
> Whatever my style of managing, am I consistent?
>
> Do I recognize that I cannot earn respect by appear-
> ing to have a participative style one day and an
> autocratic style when the going gets rough?

Coaching is one means of helping people to grow in an organizational environment. The abilities of a management team will develop only as fast as the individuals who comprise it themselves develop. We should think then of the way in which people develop.

It is recognized clearly now that the greatest single influence on a man's development is his experience as a job holder. This means that we cannot achieve development in others by 'doing things to them'. Courses, training and so on have their place, but they are a minor influence compared with what is learned through having responsibility for a job. We should therefore concentrate more effort on the creation of work situations in which people gain experience, and thus learn, rather than on developing new courses or off-the-job training experiences.

From this follows the proposition, now widely accepted, that the best form of development is self-development. This implies the recognition that the process of development is a highly individual matter. What is good for one man may be ineffective for another. We need to tailor the learning experiences

5

to the needs of each person. This is difficult for a training department to accomplish for they cannot possibly know each individual in such intimate detail. The man and his boss together should be capable of developing learning situations for the man by discussing new approaches to old tasks or by assigning new responsibilities to the subordinate. The role of the training department is to ensure that a system or framework exists within which such development can take place. The time has come for training departments to be more concerned with the development of individual managers. Unfortunately too many managers take the attitude that the training department can assume responsibility for the development of managers. It is not uncommon for a manager to say to a training man, "So-and-so needs developing, what are you going to do about it?" Too often the training man is so flattered that a manager actually has asked for his help, that he forgets to say, "Nothing—What are you, his manager, going to do?"

We accept now that manager development is for everyone. The day of the 'crown-prince' has gone. Too many people know that Abraham Lincoln was a 'failure' in his early life and that Winston Churchill did badly at school. Even the 11+ examination has come under attack as rejecting many who would have profited from a grammar school curriculum. There is no need to stress that everyone has a right to development if it is accepted that development is essentially self-development. It is up to the individual to profit from his work experience. It is up to his manager to encourage him to do so and to put opportunities in his way. Fortunately most people derive satisfaction from doing a good job, particularly if they are interested in what they are doing. Unfortunately once a job has been mastered, and the challenge has gone, tedious repetition often leads to frustration and boredom. It is the duty of managers to present new challenges to their subordinates. This is the crux of the manager development, for in accepting a new challenge the man will learn from actual experience.

This emphasis on on-the-job development focuses attention on the fact that the development of managers is primarily to equip them for today's tasks, not for some job in the future. If a man is developing consistently in today's job he will eventually outgrow it and be ready for promotion. If promotion is not available within his organization he will look elsewhere. One may doubt therefore the utility of those organizational charts which have spaces for the next occupant of a position. Such an approach appears to be too mechanical. Surely it is the merest chance if a man develops at precisely the right speed which equips him to be capable of filling the position which someone foretold for him and at the moment it becomes vacant? The reality in most organizations is that as vacancies occur those men are considered who are deemed to be suitable for filling them. Today the new job holder is rarely the man who waited for 'dead men's shoes'. In large organizations all that is required is a mechanism which ensures that all possible suitable for promotion are considered when a position has to be filled. This is to ensure equity. In practice the man who gets the job is the man whose face fits best and even then you do not know if he will succeed until he's had a chance to perform.

This is particularly true of the man who is promoted from a function to become a general manager. A good sales director does not necessarily make a good managing director. Success as a planning engineer does not necessarily prepare a man to become a works manager. A man's success in a higher post often depends on the encouragement he received from his previous manager to equip himself for increased responsibilities. This can be achieved by guiding his reading, giving him special projects or delegating more authority to him. If an organization finds itself short of up-and-coming talent it needs to question closely the abilities of the existing managers to develop their subordinates.

It will profit an organization little to encourage managers to delegate more, and so help to develop their subordinates, unless it does itself delegate responsibility to those managers who are expected to pass down part of their own responsibilities: if not, it stultifies the development of the more senior managers. They also have a right to a rewarding job! Thus the development of an organization's potential depends in part on its ability to ensure that all the important and interesting decisions are not made centrally by an oligarchy.

Throughout this book reference is made to style in management and to the importance of objectives in coaching. Clearly one cannot coach effectively if one is an autocrat for it is difficult to engage in a dialogue with autocrats.

But what is an autocrat and does he really exist in our working environment? Perhaps we use the term too glibly to vent our frustration when someone in authority turns down our pet ideas. Consider the Victorian entrepreneur, say a mill owner. Here is the archetypal autocrat—but most of them were much less so in reality. Many were fine natural coaches, going on the shop floor and discussing points of detail with their workmen, often taking off their coats to demonstrate exactly what they meant. By contrast I know many a manager who preaches participation but who behaves like an autocrat. So we should be careful about applying labels to people. Management style is a personal matter and there is no one style which enables a man to be an effective coach. What is important is that he should earn respect. In a period of great change in social thinking and aspirations it is important to know how respect is earned. To a great extent young managers are influenced by the values of their bosses in the same way that children reflect the values of their parents. So the importance a manager attaches to the *way* in which results are achieved will have an influence on the young manager. If results are to be gained at any cost then eventually the subordinate will adopt the same values. Few would accept now the following propositions:

> *that the means justifies the end*
> *that what is good for a business is always good for*
>   *the community*
> *that men are only interested in their wage packet*
> *that a successful career can only be built at the*
>   *expense of family life.*

Yet how many managers set an example to those at the start of their careers by appearing to subscribe to one or more of these propositions? One of the major influences a good coach can bring to bear upon his subordinate is to ensure that his values are likely to be relevant to the last quarter of the twentieth century. Too many young people reject a career in industry because they reject what they believe to be the values of managers, and thus the values of industry itself. We can sympathize with them even if we know them to be wrong. One doesn't improve something by remaining outside it. On the other hand, if, as a community, we are to derive the full benefit of our industrial potential then industry must learn to subscribe to the values of the community it serves. This is more than asking for statements of faith from boards of directors. If the gap between what we believe to be right and what we do in practice is to be narrowed, then it is up to every manager, who takes his coaching role seriously, to demonstrate that he attaches as much importance to the means of achieving the objectives as to their actual attainment. In this context coaching implies imparting knowledge when needed, developing skills and changing attitudes, so that a man may improve his performance. Successful coaching, as we shall see, depends on the ability to help a man to think for himself, rather than to supply answers, to do his thinking for him, or even to 'teach' him in the classroom sense of that word.

Other means of manager development can supplement the efforts of a coach, but they can never be an effective substitute for the day to day contact and help which any good leader should provide for his subordinates. To quote McGregor:[1] *:

> Every encounter between a superior and subordinate involves learning of some kind for the subordinate. (It should involve learning for the superior, too, but that is another matter). When the boss gives an order, asks for a job to be done, reprimands, praises . . . deals with a mistake . . . or takes any other action with subordinates, he is teaching them something . . . The day by day experience on the job is so much more powerful that it tends to overshadow what the individual may learn in other settings.

This implies that all managers coach, even if they do so involuntarily. Through their coaching they have a profound influence on the behaviour, attitude, motivation and work performance of their subordinates. Because coaching is such an important aspect of any

* All references are given in full at the end of each chapter

10

manager's job they should recognize not only its importance but also the need to strive to improve their own skill as coaches. The point is well made in a Central Training Council report:[2]

> ... the increasing recognition by management trainees of the vital role of manager as coach. This relatively new description of a role that the manager has always carried is particularly important because it recognizes in principle that this is a management activity open to training as much as anything else.

Coaching is a personal activity which cannot be delegated by a manager because the bond which should exist between the manager and subordinate is as tight as that which exists between any pupil and his mentor. To divide the roles of coach and mentor is to weaken the implied authority and respect which any good manager has the right to expect from his subordinates.

Good coaching is far more than simply telling a man what to do. It should seldom have much to do with the issuing of instructions or orders. One can often recognize a poor coach by his admission that he had 'told them time and again what to do and yet they keep on making the same mistakes'. To be an effective coach it is necessary to understand how people learn. One aspect of this important subject is discussed at the beginning of the next chapter. In essence the coach provides the link between learning and doing.

It is not only 'new starters' who require this help. The need exists among experienced men if they are to develop further.

If coaching is valuable to a subordinate there are benefits to be gained by the superior manager. Managers exist because they have more responsibilities than they can reasonably be expected to perform themselves, and for which they can be held accountable personally. Therefore they are assigned subordinates to assist them. The larger the organization the more the activities which lead to success are sub-divided, so that a hierarchy of responsibilities is created. Often this is represented by an organization chart.

Normally, the lower down the organization a manager is, the greater is the proportion of his time spent on carrying out tasks which are of immediate importance to the functioning of the company. For example, if all the production workers stay away for a day then there will be no production. If all the senior managers take a day off at the same time it will probably be very inconvenient but production could continue for that day at least. Consider these two charts:

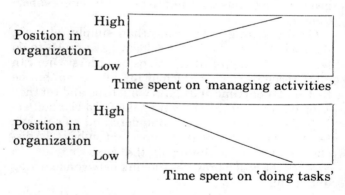

Figure 1.1

It can be seen that the higher up the organization a manager is the greater the proportion of his time is spent on managing activities (ie organizing, leading and controlling the work of others) and the less is

12

spent on 'doing' the tasks which make the organization function. At its simplest few chief executives actually arrange for the supply of raw materials, convert them into a product and then take them on the road to sell to a customer. If they do they will be operating a one man business.

Therefore, as every manager knows, he gets results through people. Put another way, if all a manager's subordinates perform well then the chances of his attaining his goals are greatly increased. In this sense a manager stands or falls on the quality of his subordinates. Because of this it is in a manager's best interests to help his subordinates to improve. Instinctively managers know this, yet so many seek panaceas for 'improving my foremen', or 'developing my management team'. A major part of the remedy lies within themselves, within their own personal competence to guide and to coach those responsible to them. Nearly all experienced supervisors are well aware of the importance of coaching. If you pass a day with such a supervisor you will find that he spends a considerable time talking to his men, discussing their work problems with them or demonstrating how he wants a job done. One of the reasons the original TWI Job Instruction programme had little effect on experienced foremen was because they could see little connection between learning how to teach a man, how to tie an electrician's knot and the practical reality of coaching on the job as they understood it. To many, TWI was a stereotyped approach which might have some value for training novices, but it had little value in helping to discuss work problems with experienced operators, and it was this aspect which was normally uppermost in the supervisor's mind.

If only senior managers had been subjected to the early TWI programmes, the lesson might have been learned sooner that good formal techniques of instructing are no substitute for day to day informal contact during which a man seeks to help a subordinate to improve by any means open to him.

If indeed managers do recognize the truth of what has been written, one may wonder why so little attention has been paid to the practice of coaching in industry and commerce. Why is it that managers do not spend more of the day consciously setting aside time to coach subordinates? There are three main causes why coaching is a recognized need but an under-utilized skill.

The first of these is apparent pressures on a manager's time. Coaching, properly conducted, is a time consuming process. It is so much simpler to 'tell' than to ask questions which will guide a man to think in a positive direction. To set aside time for coaching requires steadfastness and determination which are difficult to achieve when a manager is subjected to pressures from the telephone, his superior, and other colleagues. However, the discipline of providing time for coaching is often a major step in improving the manager's own competence. To prepare to teach is to learn oneself.

The second cause is natural shyness. Few people enjoy criticizing others to their face and managers tend to avoid conversations which may lead to open criticism of the person to whom they are talking. Thus, to many, coaching tends to become equated with 'telling' or 'teaching something new', whereas higher levels of coaching should be concerned with modification of attitudes, correction of marginally poor behaviour or, in extreme cases, creating a recognition that performance needs to be improved radically. Because managers recognize that blustering or bullying tactics will not achieve the results desired, and that, conversely, tactful hints seldom seem to work, most managers only tackle this type of conversation as a last resort, and with varying degrees of success. In most cases they tend to do most of the talking when, in fact, success is likely to lie in doing most of the listening. One cannot tell a man to improve, or order him to change his attitude, or to become more cooperative. The will to do these things stems from the man himself. The aim of coaching should be to help a man to understand the need for a desirable change. He will do this most readily if he is encouraged to think through the problem and to suggest solutions. Thus coaching is concerned more with asking questions which help a man to think, than with teaching him what to do. Once managers come to understand this they will find much of the unpleasantness they associate with 'criticizing' will be replaced by a more constructive conversation during which they as well as their subordinate will learn something.

The third cause lies in the complexity of modern organizations. Industry, as we know it, is based on notions of forecasting, planning, organizing, leading and controlling. Great emphasis is often placed on 'leading' and there have been, over the years, many analyses of what qualities are possessed by great leaders. This emphasis on leadership has been confused with 'telling' people what to do. 'Management must manage' has too often been used as an excuse for taking unpopular or even poor decisions. Yet managers do not manage in the sense of being all-powerful or in the knowledge that they only have to speak and will therefore be obeyed. A moment's reflection from your own experience will show the truth of this. An industrial community depends for its success on the balancing of many factors, not least among them the delicate relationships that exist between the goals of the organization (as an entity), the personal goals of

15

those working within it, and the often conflicting goals of the various groups of people who together make up the personnel on the company's payroll. In such a situation it is impossible to believe that in today's society a manager only has to speak and instantly he will be followed. Yet much of our industrial thinking appears to be based on this belief. How else could we cheerfully advocate appraisal systems in which men are judged by their superiors, control systems which are used only to determine whether a man has done well or badly, or any of the other techniques which are often used impersonally to alter the course of men's lives? Society, the law, trade unions and common sense are now forming a powerful combination which will finally extinguish the Victorian ethic that 'management manages'.

It is equally untrue that unions, or any other body, manage the affairs of a company. Indeed managers only in moments of exasperation have suggested that unions have asserted this right. Today a strong relationship of mutual respect and regard is growing up between union leaders (including shop stewards) and managers. Proposed changes are now commonly discussed well in advance of action, but there is often trouble if prior discussion has not taken place. Unfortunately the same regard is not always paid by superior managers in their dealing with more junior managers. Here we are only gradually breaking away from practices which imply that orders will be given and are to be obeyed. In such a situation coaching, as we understand it, is unlikely to flourish. An expert coach does not tell, he questions; he does not give orders, he explains and listens carefully to other views; to him pre-judgement is anathema; he is willing and eager to change his mind in the light of new facts, however inconvenient they may be; he has little use for a snap judgement or hasty decision on important issues. Above all he is relaxed and patient.

If this description of an effective coach seems to be 'idealistic' then it is only confirmation of how far we need to develop our ideas before we can hope to utilize our human resources effectively. It is a matter of constant surprise how much time senior managers are willing to spend discussing something with a union leader, and how often they spare only a few minutes to discuss the same subject with foremen or middle managers.

Because managers at all levels tend to reflect the attitudes and behaviour of their bosses in their own dealings with their subordinates, the style of management adopted by a chief executive has a great bearing on whether there exists, within the organization, a climate which would allow an effective coaching system to develop. However, we are not saying that coaching is impossible in an autocratic environment. To a large extent each manager can determine, if he has the will, the style of management he wishes to adopt. As coaching is an intensely personal activity, it depends on a man's personal behaviour, on the manager's determination to create time for it, and on his belief that it will make a positive contribution to his own success as a manager. It lies within the power of each manager to decide whether or not he will make a conscious attempt to improve his skills as a coach. This is of necessity a personal decision. The organization, or his own superior manager, may encourage him—he can never be forced to be an effective coach against his will.

Coaching is not a technique. Some principles can be examined and tested in practice. Proficiency, as in all things, is gained by constant practice. However, coaching provides the essential missing link in so many schemes that attempt to improve the performance of individual managers.

1 MCGREGOR D, *The Human Side of Enterprise*, McGraw-Hill, 1960
2 *Survey on Management Training and Development*, Department of Employment, 1971

CHAPTER 2

The concepts underlying coaching

The following chapters discuss what the individual manager needs to do if he is to become a successful coach. At this stage we consider in some detail half a dozen of the more important concepts which support a realistic approach to coaching.

Most of an individual's development takes place on the job

Every manager knows the importance of practical experience in acquiring new skills. It is only by trying things out in practice that we learn. Reading, listening to lectures, or working in simulated situations may help to stimulate our thoughts, or even teach us to avoid the worst mistakes; what really creates progress in our career patterns is the achievement of some goal or the overcoming of some challenge. To agree with a speaker who says "Real development is self-development" is to recognize that we probably learned more by discovering for ourselves a means to achieve a particular result than by attending courses or by reading.

Consider your own case. Perhaps you do not consciously devote time to coaching your subordinates. Progress in coaching can be achieved only by constant practice. You can become aware of the benefits of coaching and be equipped to provide them. This, however, will not make you a good coach. Only constant practice, and a determination to improve your coaching skills, will do that. A success or failure does not mean that you are able to coach well, or that you will never be able to coach. Experience on the job takes time and involves the slow overcoming of obstacles and the gradual development of expertise. Success in anything requires a determination to succeed as well as a hundred and one minor improvisations and innovations which together will bring achievement. You alone can undertake this gradual process and no course, no exhortation, no book can do more than encourage you to begin.

Learning on the job implies having a demanding job to perform

Cynics sometimes point out that 20 years' experience may mean one year's experience repeated 20 times. Unfortunately they are right, so that we must modify the concept that on-the-job experience is all that is required for a man to develop. The missing ingredient is ensuring that the job a man is asked to do makes demands on his resourcefulness and his capacity to innovate. It is the challenge of having some problem to overcome which encourages the search for new methods, or experimentation with new ideas. A prerequisite for self-development is having a challenge to be overcome. The maintenance of the *status quo* will not provide the necessary stimulus to learn or to improve skills and knowledge.

The managing director of a company which had 10 divisions dispersed throughout Britain was discussing the need for introducing a management development programme. Each division employed about 250 people and the whole enterprise was profitable—at least the Managing Director was satisfied with the return on capital employed. This man was a realist. He saw no point in a management development programme for his managers because they achieved the results he wanted. He was concerned about developing their replacements because many of the existing top team were nearing retiring age. The question he was asking himself was how could he coach young men to acquire the experience of his present team, without also engendering in them a desire to change everything and try to introduce new ideas and procedures which he would not understand or feel able to control.

The feeling that change sometimes is undertaken merely for its own sake and that this may not be in the best interests of the enterprise, should not be confused with the need to identify problems and challenges which, if surmounted, will enhance the wellbeing of the company. All organizations have problems and challenges. Their identification can be a first step in providing a demanding job for executives who need a stimulus to acquire new skills or knowledge. The problem facing the managing director cited above, was not how to develop new managers, but rather whether he was prepared to face new possibilities for his company. Unless he was prepared to accept a more demanding job, there was little point in worrying about management development schemes for his subordinates. Similarly there is no point in coaching subordinates unless we are also prepared to face the fact that they may have ideas and suggestions which are inconvenient or which demand thought and enterprise on our part. On the other hand, if we do not help our subordinates to develop, experience shows that we are likely to have a major job in covering up their inadequacies.

Managers influence the behaviour of their subordinates

That managers influence the behaviour of their subordinates would appear to be a self-evident truth, but if this were a generally understood and accepted fact many managers would modify immediately their behaviour towards their subordinates. In terms of behaviour the manager who is autocratic or bureaucratic, relaxed or demanding, well organized or disorganized, tends to breed subordinates who exhibit the same traits to a greater extent. Paradoxically many managers who exhibit in their own behaviour traits which are generally accepted to be undesirable are often the first to criticize similar behaviour in their subordinates.

There was once a works manager who each morning on arrival sent for his superintendent and gave him a good telling off; the superintendent left the office and got hold of his foreman and bawled him out; the foreman in turn shouted at one of his craftsmen, who in turn made things unpleasant for the apprentice. Having no human he could shout at, the apprentice kicked the work's cat. One day a consultant pointed out to the works manager that this daily routine cost the company money in terms of wasted energy and time. The works manager agreed and thenceforward on arriving at his works started the day by kicking the work's cat.

Apocryphal, of course, but not unbelievable except for the happy change in behaviour exhibited by the works manager. Few managers are willing to recognize that their attitudes, their priorities or their interests have a major influence on the attitudes, priorities and interests of subordinates.

A senior manager became interested in Management by Objectives. He introduced this approach to management without recognizing the importance of the leadership role he must accept if success was to be achieved. It was true that all his subordinates now had targets, controls and priorities, but these often appeared to be of secondary importance compared with the emphasis the manager appeared to place on cleanliness and neatness. Why was this? Because every time the manager appeared on the shop floor the first thing he discussed was the cleanliness and tidiness of the department. Let there be one truck outside a white line area ... The result was that foremen tended to place major emphasis on tidiness and somewhat less on other matters.

Put another way, subordinates quickly recognize what the boss thinks is really important and modify their own behaviour to keep in line. This implies that it is within the competence of managers to create expectations of high performance which their subordinates will strive to fulfil, provided that they see that the boss is consistent and reasonable in his expectations.

We shall be returning to the question of reasonable expectation in more detail in chapter 10 when we examine the relationship between coaching and performance appraisal. At this point we wish only to emphasize that a manager who appears to his subordinates to be inconsistent or unreasonable is hardly likely to be an influence for the better on the behaviour of his subordinates. Nevertheless these managers exert an influence on their subordinates. We are all aware of what may happen 'down the line' when the managing director decides to have a quality drive, or to cut costs overall by 10 per cent, or has just had a particularly difficult telephone conversation with an irate but very important customer. Irrational behaviour at the top breeds irrational behaviour lower down. Because one of the purposes of coaching is to improve the quality of subordinate decision and action, it is important that coaches should be willing to re-examine the rationality of their own actions.

Subordinates need to participate in setting objectives

In 1967 Locke and Bryan[1] showed that a person's statement of his goals and how he intended to achieve them were good predictors of his actual performance in a situation. But as Edward E Lawler III has written[2]:

> The strength of a person's motivation to perform correctly is most directly reflected in his effort; that is, in how hard he works ... at least two factors must be right if effort is to be converted into performance. First, the person must possess the necessary abilities in order to perform the job well ... A second factor ... is the person's perception of how his effort can best be converted into performance.

Good intentions are not enough. A man must possess relevant knowledge and also the skill to convert knowledge into action which will result in the achievement of his objectives. The acquisition of knowledge is the province of education and training; the development of skills to achieve action should be the result partly of experience but more importantly of discussion, guidance and help from others. And the manager is best equipped to provide this help.

The best way to attain the twin objectives of being able to monitor the actions of others without unduly restricting their freedom of action is to work closely with subordinates in setting objectives. The skills of coaching which we examine in later chapters are exactly those skills which the manager requires if his objective setting meeting is to be productive; for these skills enable the boss to ensure that both he and his subordinate agree on the same objectives and have the same views on how the subordinate's job should be done. This demands more of the manager than of the subordinate because the former needs to control a natural tendency to assume that the best way of doing a job is his own way. Part of his skill as a coach is in recognizing that even if a subordinate sets about his tasks in a manner different from that which he would have adopted, this does not imply that the subordinate will fail.

The objective setting process has the dual purpose of directing and motivating a man to achieve agreed results, and of ensuring that these results are realistic within the context of wider organizational goals. But here are the seeds of conflict, for the objectives a man may wish to achieve or which he sees to be necessary, are not necessarily the same which his manager or the organization recognizes as priorities.

A young salesman who was keen and enthusiastic was more than willing to participate in the setting of his own objectives. He was well aware that sales volume and revenue earned were the key areas of his responsibility. He was gratified to find that his area sales manager also recognized the importance of these two factors. What he found much less acceptable was the area manager's view that he should concentrate not only on the lines which were easy to sell, but also on those which would enhance the reputation of the company in the market place as being suppliers of a range of goods of high quality and competitive price. Many area sales managers would content themselves with giving this brief explanation of the need for a more balanced sales performance; this man, however, spent much time and effort asking questions which led the salesman to appreciate for himself why concentration on a limited product range was not in the best long term interest of the company or of is employees.

Managers should discipline themselves to ensure that the objective setting situation is one where learning takes place, for real acceptance of an objective is only given when a man has convinced himself that the objective is worth striving for.

Control information must be available

We learn from the mistakes we make; we strive to improve because we recognize that we can do better. It follows that we need information to assess how well we have been doing, and to recognize what scope there is likely to be for further improvement. Any manager who takes the trouble to work out with his subordinates the goals towards which he wishes them to strive should also ensure that control information is available to them through which they can monitor their performance.

The subordinate should not just be spoon-fed with information. Encouraging a man to set up his own simple controls by which he can judge for himself what is happening is often more effective in terms of stimulating corrective action, than pages of computer print-outs presented on a weekly basis. This is a lesson which many foremen have learned for themselves. In our experience a good supervisor will often prepare 'simple to keep' graphs or tables in his office, even when computer print-outs are available to him. There is a good deal to be said for this because the act of preparing one's own information often focuses attention on those matters which require attention.

However, preparing one's own control information is only likely to be valuable (and not a time consuming exercise) if the information which is being tabulated or graphed is within one's own control. For example, preparing a table of overtime hours worked is a simple exercise if the time-sheets pass through the foreman's office. If some other method of time recording is used then it should be thought necessary to inform the foreman of the overtime worked as soon after the event as possible. Only in this way can he be encouraged to take corrective action.

Shortening the time-scale between an event taking place, and its recognition by the person responsible, is a major factor in encouraging self-control. Far too often a great deal of information is made available which, though accurate, arrives too late to enable action to be taken.

The question of what control information a man requires to monitor his performance, and how it should be prepared, is an important topic for coaches to discuss with their subordinates. Most of us are often so immersed in the details of carrying out our tasks that we forget the importance of monitoring what we are doing. This exemplifies the difference between being busy (performing activities) and taking time to assess what has been achieved and what requires to be done (managing).

A foreman in a continuous process plant was always active, spending a good proportion of his time on the shop floor. He was convinced that he knew what went on, and in times of stress he was always there to give a helping hand. One day he was asked how much time was lost every week through his machines being idle. Although he admitted that he kept no figures, he stated categorically that little unavoidable time was lost because he was always there to investigate the cause of any unexpected breakdown or lost time. Experimentally he agreed to keep figures of all lost time for one week. He did the recording himself. At the end of three days he was horrified to find that 30 per cent of his possible productive hours had been lost through down time. Each occurrence had a seemingly justifiable cause, but the foreman was so perturbed that he started to change a number of working practices. Three months later the lost time in his department was reduced to 10 per cent and he had saved his company many thousands of pounds.

The important part of this story is that the foreman was persuaded to build up his own control information. It is more effective to learn things for ourselves than to be given facts which we may question.

It is not always possible to build up for oneself all the control information required. This is especially true when working as part of a group. Even in these cases superior managers should strive to make control information available to all members of the group as soon as possible after an agreed compilation date. It is as true for groups as for individuals that the speed with which the results of action are known has an important bearing on the impact of the information given.

Frequent informal contact between men is more valuable than infrequent formal contact

Frequency of contact between the manager and subordinate is an important factor in coaching. We know of a number of cases where subordinates seldom meet their managers, though happily these instances are few. More common, unfortunately, are situations where manager and subordinate often meet but the subordinate gains little understanding of his superior manager's views. In these instances there is little real communication between the two men and it is left to the junior partner to guess whether his behaviour and actions meet with approval.

We all know of cases where men have said that they supposed that they were doing all right because no one had complained. The trouble is that complaints tend to be made behind a man's back instead of to his face. The increasingly wide recognition of this truth led to the adoption of appraisal systems. The wish of subordinates to be 'told how they were doing' is one of the five needs of a manager postulated by John Humble.[3] Unfortunately this advance has, in many superior/subordinate relationships, led to each side storing up the real expression of their views until the formal appraisal meeting occurs. This is not to decry the value of such meetings. They are infinitely better than doing nothing at all, and a degree of formality, or stocktaking, between manager and managed is to be encouraged as we will see in chapter 10.

Much more is required, however, than infrequent formal meetings if true coaching is to take place. Just as the manager influences subordinate behaviour by his management style, so does he encourage his subordinate to develop by the way in which he uses his day-to-day opportunities to coach.

This day-to-day coaching is time consuming because it demands the ability to ask questions which are designed to help the subordinate to think through a problem for himself, rather than to supply ready-made answers. These ready-made answers often take the form of instructions which leave the subordinate little room for manoeuvre, and less opportunity for learning for himself. Thus, as we have frequent cause to remark, there is a definite connection between management style and the ability to coach well. Too formal, or too autocratic a style will inhibit the subordinate's desire to think for himself, except in terms of doing those things which will keep him out of trouble. This is the antithesis of coaching which demands a free interchange of views between two men.

The successful coach, then, is on the look-out continually for opportunities to help his subordinate to develop his own thinking. Such opportunities are there for the grasping provided he takes time to recognize them. Here are a few situations which frequently can develop into an informal coaching session:

> *The subordinate asks a question. 'How do I do this?' 'whom shall I consult?' 'Is this course of action satisfactory?' The coach who declines to give a straight answer but asks further questions is helping his subordinate to think the matter through. A situation occurs which demands the superior's intervention. Does he issue an order or ask testing questions designed to lead the subordinate to suggest the correct course of action?*
>
> *A man goes on a course or seminar. Is he told to go, or does a full discussion take place relating to the probable value of his attendance? Similarly, is he asked for his ideas on return from the course?*
>
> *During preparation for an important meeting does the manager lecture the subordinate, or does he take time to seek his views and guide his thinking by further questioning?*

Opportunities like these provide the basis of a sound relationship between two men which in time will strengthen the bond between them and improve the quality of their joint contribution to the enterprise.

The difference between counselling and coaching

At this stage it is necessary to define more precisely what we understand to be the difference between counselling and coaching because our experience indicates that often 'counselling' is used to include what we would define more exactly as a 'coaching' process. It is important that practising managers should be clear about the distinction because their capacity to evolve into effective *coaches* depends to some extent upon their recognition that counselling is a different process which, though important, requires somewhat different skills and attitudes, or at least a changed emphasis and use of the skills and attitudes displayed by a coach.

Counselling has to do with helping and giving advice to the individual, whilst coaching is more a joint process through which the coach is as likely to learn as much as is the person he is coaching. Counselling in industry often takes place at two levels—assistance with personal problems which arise outside the company, and advice of a personal nature which is intended to help a man to enhance his career or to fit himself better for the post he currently occupies.

Counselling of the first type, dealing with personal problems, is a dangerous area for any manager unless he happens to be a professionally trained social worker. Probably more harm has been done by well meaning attempts by the unqualified to help those in trouble, than the unconcern of a manager who says 'personal problems should not be brought to work'. The correct course, and we state this unequivocally, for a manager who wishes to help an employee who has a personal problem is to afford him time off to seek professional advice. If there is a personnel department its staff should be able to refer the employee to an appropriate source of help, probably outside the company. If no personnel department exists the local Citizens' Advice Bureau may be able to assist. A few larger companies employ professionally qualified welfare officers to whom any employee with personal problems can be referred.

By far the greater area in which counselling takes place is that of advice on career prospects and how an employee can improve in his present post.

Most of us, particularly in the early stages of our careers, like to talk to our bosses about our career prospects, although a cynic might agree with John Collins that "to ask advice is in nine cases out of 10 to tout for flattery". However, it is flattering to be asked one's advice and the range of answers we give varies from 'read this book', 'attend that course' to 'seek another post in order to gain wider experience'. In the end, of course, the recipient of our pearls of wisdom makes up his own mind and we can be cut down to size by the reflection that he has only used us as a chopping-block in order to clarify his own thoughts. If we have helped a man in this way we have certainly performed a useful function.

Too often, however, counselling of this type degenerates into the more dangerous practice of playing god. Here we enter the realms of telling a man what we think it is good for him to know. Typical examples are:

> *If you want to get on you should take more care of your appearance*
> *You seem incapable of getting on with people—try to become more tactful—less abrasive*
> *Can't you see that if the boss works late, it's wise for you to work late as well.*

and in one supreme example of arrogance by a manager to a subordinate:

I think if I were you I'd move to a better area of town.

It is wise, therefore, for those who feel impelled to offer counsel to others to ask themselves whether they do so from a genuine desire to help, or perhaps only from a natural tendency, present in everyone, to wish to offer advice.

Coaching, on the other hand, seeks to help a man to find solutions to work problems. Because no man works in isolation, the solution of a particular work problem will be in modified behaviour, or new lines of action, taken by others beside himself. The boss who wishes to coach should therefore recognize that far from 'playing god', 'advising' or 'telling' he is in reality a partner in a catalytic process through which both he and his subordinate will find solutions to the work problems which beset them.

To sum up, a coach needs to recognize that:

it is experience on the job which teaches most, and that he can influence considerably the benefit which subordinates can gain from their work experience

the way jobs are structured influences the amount of learning which takes place, and that a manager has considerable scope to create new challenges

as a manager his example influences the attitudes, behaviour and development of those in his command

if subordinates participate in the setting of their objectives then they will be more committed to their attainment and will be stimulated to learn

learning in part depends on knowing whether our efforts have met with success, so subordinates require control information to monitor their performance coaching is a continuing process which cannot be fully effective if carried out only at predetermined intervals

counselling and coaching are different processes. The latter is a catalytic process in which both men learn.

1 LOCKE E A and BRYAN J F, *Goals and Intentions as Determinants of Performance Level Task Choice and Attitudes,* American Institute for Research, Washington.
2 LAWLER EDWARD E III, Job Attitudes and Employee Motivation Theory, Research And Practice, *Personnel Psychology,* 1970.
3 HUMBLE J, *Improving Management Performance,* British Institute of Management, 1965

CHAPTER 3

The subordinate's needs in the coaching process

If the coaching process is to achieve results which are to be of benefit both to the subordinate and to his manager, it is important for the manager to bear in mind a number of points which will enable both men to derive maximum advantage from their discussions. Let us consider some aspects for which the coach bears the major, but certainly not all the responsibility.

The supervisor and subordinate should have the same objectives

Managers do not exist to maintain the *status quo* but rather to co-ordinate the efforts of others in seeking a means to achieve improvement. At the top of a company these aspirations may be incorporated in a corporate plan. At lower levels they should take the form of unit or individual objectives. Before effective coaching can take place there must be broad agreement between the superior and subordinate as to the objectives which the coaching is designed to achieve. These objectives will normally be expressed in terms of work objectives such as:

> *an improved cost control system*

more thorough penetration of a market area by salesmen
greater reliability in a production process
improved labour relations in a department.

Objectives such as these are too generalized to be of value unless they are accompanied by identified tasks through which the wider objective will be achieved. Also an action plan is needed for carrying out the tasks and it is necessary to identify standards of performance which enable the degree of success achieved to be measured. To be of value the identification of tasks, action to be taken and standards for success must be integrated both with corporate objectives *and* with what is deemed realistic by the job holder. The manager must seek, therefore, the views of the job holder before finalizing the objectives for which he will hold him responsible. The difficulty of this process arises from the problems of reconciling the differing aspirations of the job holder and of his boss, and the needs of the company. For some managers the solution is clear in the style of management they adopt. Put crudely this can be stated as:

work out at the top what is needed and communicate this down the line in terms of unit and individual objectives.

Coaching has little part to play in this although 'training' or 'conditioning' people may be important if people are to acquire the skills they need.

Society tends to react against such crude manipulation of people. Most of us resent being told what to do; we expect to play a part in building up the objectives for which we are to be held accountable. Furthermore we are able readily to see through insincere attempts to cloak the naked imposition of objectives by meetings designed to communicate, or to explain, what is to be done. We expect our own views to have a real influence on the decisions made, although we are often willing to accept the broad strategy arrived at through a searching analysis of the business problems of the organization.

The coaching process, therefore, starts with the reconciliation of the objectives of the manager with those of his subordinate. Its aim must be to ensure that both men are striving for the same things. The successful coach will be able to:

help his subordinate understand the reasons why certain objectives must be achieved

modify his own original view of how these overall objectives can be met by taking into account the views of his subordinate

ensure that the work for which the subordinate is to be responsible is within his knowledge or capacity to perform.

This last point implies that although, where possible, subordinates should be given new tasks or responsibilities which 'stretch' them, care must be taken to ensure that they have adequate opportunity, resources and guidance to learn any new knowledge or skills required.

The coach must allow the subordinate to feel he has responsibility

All of us feel that we know the best method of tackling a job, particularly those which involve tasks with which we have had great experience. The danger is that we may fail to recognize that the same results can frequently be achieved by adopting a different approach or style from the one with which we feel at ease or with which we are familiar. If we are not aware of this then we are likely to stifle the subordinate's initiative and to wrest from him the very responsibility and confidence which we wish to encourage.

We should not seek to ensure that he adopts a working method which is the image of our own. Subordinates observe their superiors closely. They will copy those aspects of style and approach to tackling problems which they feel to be valuable, but will experiment with their own ideas in areas where they feel a new approach would be desirable. Sometimes these ideas of their own will fail, but the experiment will have been worthwhile because the men may have learned something from their failures. When a new approach is successful then both the man, his manager and the organization benefit.

The following case history illustrates how one manager successfully trod the narrow path between allowing a man to flounder helplessly and providing such detailed guidance that the subordinates initiative was stifled.

A young manager in a large company was asked to investigate a quality control problem in his own department. His superior manager spent several hours, spread over a week, helping the young man to plan his investigation. He asked questions which led the man to draw up a comprehensive list of facts which he would need to assemble. The man was then left to carry out the investigation. Four weeks later he had drawn up a draft report which he took to his manager. It contained the basis for what seemed to be worthwhile action, but was poorly written and the facts were incompletely marshalled. The superior manager spent several more hours of questioning which led the young man to want to rewrite the report. The second attempt was much better, but still required improvement which was now provided by the superior manager. The final report was

accepted and the young manager was given respon-
sibility for introducing the changes recommended.
He managed this successfully and the savings
amounted to £3000 in the first year. The young
manager grew in competence and is today a senior
manager. In conversation he pays tribute to the way
in which his superior manager helped him to
develop; working for that particular manager
taught him a great deal, not only about his job but
how to coach his own subordinates in later years.

The subordinate must be encouraged to ask questions

In chapter 6 we deal more fully with the skills of listening and questioning. At this point the importance of encouraging the subordinate to ask questions and to solve problems for himself must be emphasized. The skilful coach adopts a balance between giving all the necessary information and allowing the man to waste too much time discovering the correct approach to a problem. Discovery learning is all very well—but one needs a minimum basis of knowledge with which to discover.

John Humble, for instance, is a skilful coach. He never asks a man to work on a problem without discussing with him the way in which a solution can be structured. Initially he will talk and write down headings for a suitable approach. He always stops short of giving a total approach so that the paper on which the notes have been written is liberally scattered with 'etc'.

This is one method of ensuring that the subordinate has sufficient basic guidelines on which to build. The very incompleteness of the ideas supplied by the coach will spark off further ideas in the coached. It is at this stage that the man should be encouraged to ask questions and so to begin to develop his own thinking.

Some ideas put forward may appear to the coach to be irrelevant or off-beam. But if the man has thought of them they are worthy of consideration. Perhaps they require more investigation, and this should be stated. Other ideas need elaboration to assure the coach that the subordinate has grasped the real nature of the problem to be solved. Further questioning on the part of the coach should enable him to draw out the subordinate and to help him appreciate what is required.

The following is a working basis for giving a subordinate new responsibilities or tasks:

state the task and the reason first
give enough basic information and ideas to enable the man to begin to formulate his own ideas
encourage the man to ask questions and to state his initial reactions
do not stamp on statements or thoughts with which you disagree. All ideas are worth considering. They are made in good faith and a little work on them may germinate an idea unperceived or unacknowledged before.

Learning takes time

Some people learn faster than others. None of us appreciates at the first attempt the full significance of something new. Most problems in organizations are complex enough to demand carefully thought out, rather than off-the-cuff solutions. Coaches need to appreciate this and allow sufficient time for the full implications of new ideas to be recognized.

It is common for a manager or group of managers to spend weeks or months discussing possible ways of solving a problem and then to communicate the fruits of their thinking to subordinates in one short meeting. They are then appalled when what to them now appears to be a straightforward solution, is received with less than enthusiasm. They forget that others have not had the benefit of being required to think through the problem in depth for themselves.

The coach is often in a similar position. He should recognize that the skill of analysing problems and formulating possible solutions may not be so highly developed in those being coached as himself because they have less experience. We all pay a great deal of respect to experience. In many cases it is valuable—in every case it has taken time to accumulate. One of the objectives of a coach is to transmit his worthwhile experience to others, to shorten the time it would take for them to learn the same things for themselves. However, a year of experience cannot be assimilated in an hour or two, even if it could be transmitted in that time. So some useful guidelines are:

initially give enough information to enable the man to work on the problem

supplement the information at intervals in answer to questions when the man makes his periodic reports

try to restrict the giving of information to those aspects which the man sees as relevant. This will ensure that you are not telling him more than he can absorb.

Check that the learner comprehends fully what is being discussed

It is easy to assume that a listener understands fully what he hears. Everyone knows those people who expound their views at great length, hardly pausing for breath, and certainly exhibiting little real interest in the reactions of their audience provided that they nod or make appropriate noises of agreement at regular intervals. Interruptions or questions are brushed aside as quickly as possible so that the speaker can return to the mainstream of his own ideas. The real learner in this sort of situation is the speaker, for the process of expounding his ideas helps him to develop them.

The clue to the process of checking on comprehension by a listener lies in allowing him to develop ideas first propounded by the speaker. In this way he will not only demonstrate that he has followed the argument put forward but, more importantly, he will have the opportunity of reinforcing the ideas he has heard by supplementing them with his own thoughts. Thus both the listener and the speaker learn, and the coach has an opportunity to discover whether his subordinate really understands the wider implications of the subject matter under discussion. In a coaching situation the coach should not seek for a parrot-like feed back or précis of what he has said. Rather he should try to ascertain whether his listener has understood the reasons for his statements. Such understanding cannot be tested by highly structured questions begging mere assent or dissent; it can only be revealed by the quality of the listener's contribution to the subsequent discussion. Therefore, an essential element in coaching is to encourage contributions from the subordinate as a means of checking his full comprehension of the subject matter under review.

Suppose that a manager wishes to explain to a foreman how a new production control system will work. Unfortunately, the most common method of doing this is to go through the new system asking, at regular intervals, whether a particular point is clear. This normally elicits the answer 'yes'. Any questions asked are likely to be concerned with detail and the manager will probably leave convinced that the new system is both fully understood and will be applied with enthusiasm. Experience suggests that both assumptions are less than true. The foreman on reflection will see many snags which have not been discussed even if he were asked directly "Can you see any difficulties?" Such direct challenges are likely to get a negative answer because the man has insufficient time to marshal his thoughts and to think through the full implications of the proposed changes.

A better approach would be for the manager to take more time and to involve the foreman in the build up of the thinking which led to the change in the system. After all the new procedures were not evolved overnight. Careful thought took place over a period of weeks or months. Even if it were impossible for the foreman to be consulted fully during the period of development, a wise manager should seek to help the man to understand the thought processes by which it was evolved. If the system is appropriate to the work situation then the foreman should be able, under guidance, to discover for himself why the change is required. If this is the aim of coaching then the manager needs to discuss the development of the new system with his foreman. A good starting point is to discuss with him the shortcomings of the present system and to work from there towards the way in which the new arrangements had originated and been developed. Two major advantages accrue. First, the foreman will commit himself to the need for change, and second he may think of improvements in the proposals which have not yet been thought of. The second advantage is crucial. The knowledge possessed by a manager is different from that of a man working the system. He may see problems not visualized by the manager.

The end result will be a foreman who not only understands what is now required, but is committed to the change. Thus, in a coaching situation checking on comprehension by the learner is really a process of allowing him time and opportunity under guidance to formulate a solution which is appropriate not only to his own needs, but also to the needs of the factory as a whole.

The coach must ensure that the subordinates receive a feed-back on their performance

In the context of the coaching process we are not referring to 'feed-back' in the sense of control information which was discussed in chapter 2. Although people learn when they have regular information on how they are getting on, feed-back during coaching tends to be an informal process during which the man is given encouragement to develop his own thinking.

Nothing is more discouraging than to be told, either explicitly or by inference, that one is talking nonsense. In a manager/subordinate relationship this situation can only lead to the subordinate waiting to hear what are the superior's views. He may well think them 'nonsense' as well, but will hardly say so. Unless there exists a mutual trust and understanding, which is so often absent in manager/subordinate relationships, most men will try to ascertain what are acceptable responses to their superiors' statements. This is learning, but of the wrong kind.

One of the axioms of good industrial relations is that if a group of people hold an opinion strongly and sincerely, then that opinion should be respected, understood and taken into account—even if the premise on which it is based is wrong. Similarly in the relationship between coach and coached, the opinions of the latter should be respected. To ride over them roughshod or to dismiss them summarily, only results in an apparent acquiescence in the views of the coach. Real understanding of issues by a subordinate cannot be based on such cavalier tactics. He needs to be led to an understanding of how his convictions are wrongly conceived. This can be achieved by questioning and helping the man to think things out for himself. It depends also on supplying information from which sound conclusions can be drawn. Learning in a managerial situation is largely a process of developing ideas and attitudes. Feed-back to the subordinate from the coach should be in a form which encourages the man to think more deeply because he knows that his own contributions to the discussion are seen by the coach to be relevant and helpful.

The method used should be adjusted to meet the needs of the subordinate

It should be apparent now that there are no strict rules for coaching. It is not possible to produce a checklist of steps which, if followed, will lead to the desired results. On the other hand there are a number of principles, discussed in this book, on which the would-be coach can draw and adapt to his own use.

The coach needs to adapt these principles in the light of his experience with a particular man. Some will require only a general discussion of a problem to be stimulated to read more widely about a subject, or to wish to attend a relevant course or seminar. Another man may need step-by-step coaching, conducted painstakingly over a period of weeks, to take him through the details of a new approach to a long standing problem. If the latter approach appears to be unduly time-consuming it may be worth reflecting on the amount of time which will have to be spent in the future sorting out mistakes which arise from a mistaken or an incomplete understanding of the point which is the subject of the coaching.

In adapting coaching tactics to the needs of a subordinate there is one paramount consideration which needs to be taken into account. This is the importance of helping the subordinate to learn. The coach himself requires a feed-back as to whether learning, or a desire to learn, exists. If he is successful in stimulating learning then the coach will know that he is adopting the appropriate method.

The wise coach gives credit to his subordinates

In any discussion both parties learn something and each contributes to the development of the other's thinking. It is axiomatic, therefore, that an open-minded coach is likely to learn from his subordinate. Overt recognition of this encourages the subordinate and reinforces his desire to continue to learn. A man who knows that he is contributing something useful to a discussion will strive to learn more. Therefore, without being effusive, a good coach will let his subordinate know when he has contributed helpful thinking to the joint discussion.

What coaching requires of a subordinate

People cannot be forced to develop if they do not wish to do so. They are motivated to develop by internal and external factors, and then only if they can see that such development will enable them to satisfy their own aspirations. Thus a manager, whose personal need to have responsibility is of a low level, may not want promotion even though it may bring an increase in salary or status. Fortunately most people have an inherent interest in the work they are doing although at times a cynic might ponder on whether managements do their best to frustrate this interest by ignoring a subordinate's aspirations to seek some control over his activities. Managers are often as equally insensitive to the aspirations of more junior managers and supervisors as they are to shop-floor personnel. One of the major advantages of coaching is that it demonstrates on the part of the manager a real interest in helping a subordinate to learn how to perform his job better. In most of us this is likely to strike a chord of response because we do not particularly relish spending a large proportion of our working hours in trying to perform a job which we find frustrating or lacking in interest. However, successful coaching demands that the subordinate should have a basic desire to learn. This is most likely to be present when his job objectives:

place a demand on his abilities
*appear to him to be achievable if he makes the
    necessary effort*
*appear to assist in the achievement of the total com-
    pany or work group objectives as he under-
    stands them*
*allow him sufficient responsibility so that he can
    achieve the desired results*
possess sufficient inherent interest to satisfy him.

Thus the way jobs are structured provides one basic ingredient for successful coaching. For example a supervisor who is given responsibility for results in terms of amount, quality and cost of production, but is allowed little discretion or authority over the way in which these results are to be achieved, is unlikely to derive much job satisfaction or to welcome coaching, however good it is.

Participation by the subordinate in the build up of his job objectives and the degree of authority he is allowed are very desirable prerequisites for sustained and successful coaching. Such participation does, of course, provide its own coaching opportunities. In fact even if such participation is not present when a manager begins to coach, a joint review of the man's job structure is likely to occur after a period of successful coaching.

The attitude of the subordinate to his coach is of great importance. A man is unlikely to be a good coach if he does not command the respect of his learner. Respect can only be earned, it cannot be demanded. For his part a subordinate should be prepared to seek out, and to use, the strengths of his superior manager in order that his wider knowledge or experience can be brought to bear on the work problems which are under review. Thus coaching can never be a one-way process. It always depends on the determination of both men to make the process work.

CHAPTER 4

The characteristics of good coaches

J W Riegel[1] has identified five characteristics of good coaches:

they are interested in their people
they look for potentialities
they know the interests, desires and capacities of their subordinates
their interests are person-centred rather than work-centred
they show confidence in subordinates, but expect it to be justified.

To which we can add a sixth:

they don't do all their subordinates' thinking for them.

These important characteristics are worthy of more detailed attention.

Interest in their people

To take an interest in one's subordinates is far more than an act of welfare or good manners. In many cases it may have nothing at all to do with the prying type of interest so often recommended and exemplified by personal enquiries about family or holiday plans. To some subordinates this type of questioning only provokes resentment or cynicism and is seen by them as irrelevant to their needs at work.

Real interest in the work situation demands that the boss wishes to develop his people so that they are able to think for themselves, accomplish objectives, have ambition, mature emotionally, be self-reliant and self-confident, tolerant of others and above all never cease to wish to learn. A manager can judge the effectiveness of his coaching by the extent to which his people develop these attributes. None of these can be taught in a formal sense; they develop only in an environment which allows and encourages self-development and self-criticism.

Looking for potentialities

Too often we fail to recognize that a man is capable of accomplishing a more demanding task, or assume too readily that a man who performs well can be given new tasks without training or guidance. Most individuals are capable of mastering new challenges, provided that adequate coaching, guidance and encouragement are given. Looking for a man's potentialities, therefore, implies that a manager needs to think constantly of providing new opportunities for self-development in his subordinates.

This is more than waiting for vacancies to occur in order that a man may be promoted. A manager should take the time and the trouble during the course of a subordinate's current appointment to assess his ability to cope with new and greater responsibilities. If managing is largely about meeting new challenges the manager should not lack opportunity, should he wish it, to offer his subordinates the chance to develop on their jobs. Frederick Herzberg has pointed out frequently that all work should be a learning experience. The manager who seeks out the potentialities of his subordinates is helping to create a situation in which learning and, therefore, the possibility of greater job satisfaction, can take place.

It is, of course, easier to give a new task to an established performer rather than to assign it to a man who will require help and guidance to perform it well. In the long run, however, the most effective management team will be one where there is a general high standard of all-round performers, rather than a few outstanding individuals amongst mediocrities.

They know their subordinates

A major skill in management is the capacity to understand one's subordinates. This requires the ability to get to know what encourages a man to perform well. As he is unlikely, and possibly unable, to tell you what are his real, as opposed to imagined, motivators the good boss seeks to discover for himself what is important to his man. This can be done only over a period. It demands an interest in people but, perhaps more importantly, the capacity to judge in what situations and circumstances a man is likely to perform well.

High performance does depend, of course, on the ability of an individual. Good bosses 'stack the cards' in favour of high achievement by seeking to ensure that the circumstances in which jobs are performed are the most favourable to success. A senior consultant, long since retired, exhibited this quality to the full. When he assigned men to a particular job he was careful to ensure that they were competent, but gave equal consideration to their ability to cooperate with the client's executives. He asked not only whether they fitted the job but whether they would fit in with their colleagues.

There is an increasing emphasis in modern industry and commercial practice on teamwork, on teams of managers, rather than on reliance on individual performance. A wise manager will select the managers in each team with care so that personality conflicts will not endanger success. Equally he will seek to ensure that the team as a whole is not complacent and generates new ideas. He will therefore try to include at least one member who is able and willing to challenge existing thinking.

Building teams with these and similar considerations in mind will be easier if a manager really understands how his subordinates think. One obvious way of doing this is to use the skills of listening and discussion which are discussed in chapters 6 and 7. Thus coaching is not only a means of improving delegation to individuals, it is also useful to a manager in helping him to think about the composition of teams.

Person-centred rather than work-centred

This quality of the good coach does not imply that he is interested only in people and not in work. Good coaching is work-centred just as the end product of successful coaching is improved performance on the job.

The person-centred coach is more concerned with developing his subordinate's ability to deal with problems, rather than that he should deal with them himself. It is the difference in attitude between "If you want something done it is best to do it yourself" and "This person will never learn if he is not given a chance to make mistakes". Here again, the manager requires to exercise self-discipline. It is often easier and less time-consuming to perform a task oneself rather than to spend time explaining what is required to a subordinate. The greater the pressures on a manager the more the temptation (and in some cases the necessity) for him to do-it-himself. But teams of competent people are built by giving others the opportunity to perform. Managers who really try to make this maxim a reality are agreeably surprised by the latent talent and inventiveness exhibited by those in whom they have put their trust.

A large company in the printing industry planned to introduce some new machinery into one of its departments. In the past this type of innovation had led to major labour problems relating to pay, the apportionment of work between operators, inter-union demarcation disputes and levels of manning. Additionally, in this case, it was necessary to introduce shift working in a department which had always worked a 'normal' working day. This had one advantage only—there need be no redundancy resulting from the fact that the new machinery theoretically required fewer operators than that which it replaced. The word theoretically is used because those readers who know the printing industry will recognize that de-manning arising from the introduction of new plant is often a major problem.

In the past the personnel department and senior production management had been the only participants in union negotiations about the introduction of new machinery. However, the company had negotiated a year previously a comprehensive productivity agreement which included a clause designed to facilitate the introduction of new machines. The company had had one experience of implementing this clause in another department. In that instance, when it had wanted to act, a long series of negotiations had been necessary before the old machines could be replaced.

On this occasion the personnel director suggested that the department manager be given sole responsibility for the smooth introduction of the new machinery and the introduction of shift working. There was resistance to this idea, including a look of horror on the department manager's face, for senior management had always carried out what were considered to be difficult negotiations. The personnel director pointed out that the company's previous experience in this respect had hardly been happy. With some misgivings those concerned decided to give his idea a try. His only ally at this time was the senior production manager, who approved of the innovation and played a major part in persuading the department manager that he could succeed where others had failed. The department manager was fully briefed on the details of the changes involved, and on the benefits which would arise. He made a number of constructive suggestions and discussed with his production manager and the personnel director how he should set about preparing his operators for the change. This involved him seeing them as a group and giving them full details of what was planned, including the cost benefits and the extra output which would be obtained.

The department manager was by no means satisfied with this meeting. Immediately questions of pay and manning had been raised and there was an obvious reluctance to change to shift work. He reported these results to his production manager who only asked 'Will the men be willing to talk to you again on this subject?' After the reply that they would it was agreed that the department manager would hold a series of meetings, exploring all the operators' doubts, frankly answering their queries,

54

and inviting their suggestions as to how the new machines should be introduced within the context of the productivity agreement.

A series of further meetings took place in the department. Gradually the manager gained confidence and the operators made proposals and suggestions which he felt were fair to the company, fair to the men and some of which were an improvement on the company's original plans. A number of these related to the layout and servicing of the new plant.

Throughout this period the senior production manager supported and helped his department manager by making suggestions and helping him to develop his thinking. However, the senior production manager never once attended a department meeting.

There were many alarms and excursions on the way but today that department is operating the new plant on a double day shift system with a reasonable level of manning and on pay rates which are in line with the productivity agreement. The operators feel that they played a major role in setting up the new arrangements and the department manager has increased markedly his stature as a manager.

Confidence

This case history illustrates well the characteristics of a good coach. The senior production manager grasped an opportunity to give his department manager responsibility for a major and very difficult change. He never interfered with the detailed shop floor negotiations but he was always at hand to give help and advice, or just to act as a sounding-board, when the going got tough.

Above all he was willing to display confidence in his subordinate. There is naturally a risk element in all successful coaching. No man can be certain that his subordinates will perform well, but the act of giving responsibility should imply confidence that the task set will be achieved. It is unreasonable to expect a man to give of his best if he suspects that his boss, because of his behaviour, does not really expect him to succeed and is only waiting for him to fail before doing the job himself.

Ensure that their subordinates think for themselves

It is so much easier in the short term to make decisions, and even to take action, oneself than to spend time encouraging subordinates to think through their own problems. How many times last week did your subordinates ask you a question which, with a little thought you feel they could have answered for themselves? How many times do you express a wish that your subordinates would think for themselves? The paradox is that we all like to be asked questions and to supply answers. We are all too willing to be used as a crutch by others and to do their thinking for them. Perhaps it does our 'ego' good! Good coaches ensure that their subordinates use their brains. When asked a question calling for a decision they ask "What would you suggest?"

Managers who use this approach find that their subordinates either ask them fewer questions and thus save their time (but still the subordinates make the decisions themselves), or they come prepared with reasoned choices indicating that they have thought the problem through and wish the manager to help them to come to a decision. The result is that these managers have more time to do the things that require doing, and have to spend less time

propping up their staff, or doing their job for them.
For their part the subordinates find that they are
learning a great deal and gain in confidence. Once,
you may have worked for a manager who infuriated
you by asking you questions instead of supplying
answers. Didn't you learn a lot?

The problem of course is that managers often feel
indecisive when they don't supply instant answers.
Indeed many managers acknowledge that they have
worked under bosses who appeared to be incapable of
giving decisions. On reflection, however, they have
often come to the conclusion that this was an
important formative period of their life. Perhaps
the way to avoid the imputation of being incapable
of giving a decision is to make it clear to one's
subordinates why one is making them think for
themselves.

The neatest story summing up the points made was
told by a senior manager who, in his first job, was
discussing with his boss what course of action he
should take. He gave the pros and cons on three
choices and then asked for a decision by his boss.
"No," said his boss "You've thought it through, you
choose—I'll back you." Today that manager recog-
nizes how much that boss did for his personal
development and for his confidence.

How does this differ from common management practice?

It is commonly asserted that management must
manage. A better phrase would be management must
lead. Too often the act of managing involves analysing facts, making a decision and selling or imposing
the decision on subordinates. There are occasions
when such stark simplicity is appropriate, but this

style of management can have no place in a coaching process.

Many are beginning to question whether this style of management, even when it is wrapped up in committees or consultation to sweeten the pill, is appropriate to the expectations of people in the last quarter of this century. A manager who manages this way will often get results but he may well question whether such results might not have been improved if he had been willing to utilize fully the experience, the ideas and the initiatives of his subordinates.

There is as much confusion about management style as there is about leadership. No set of rules, slavishly followed, will make a person an effective leader. Similarly, styles of management do not lend themselves to facile categorization. We think we understand the terms 'authoritarian' or 'participative'. But consider the Victorian autocrat who invited the participation of his staff in technical decisions; or consider the manager who preaches participation and turns out to be extremely autocratic in his decision making processes.

Management style is a highly personal matter. There is no technique which will aid a manager to create an environment in which subordinates' skills and knowledge are fully utilized. A sensitivity to the feelings and ideas of others can only be gained if a manager wishes to act in this way and is willing to question constantly his personal contribution in achieving an aim genuinely sought. To appear to go through the formalities of harnessing the ideas of others without really believing in the value of their contribution will soon be recognized for the sham such behaviour represents.

No manager should attempt to coach if he is unwilling, or unable, to make time to encourage his subordinates to think for themselves. If he rushes the process he may end up appearing to lose his incisiveness; his subordinates, who have relied on him for decisions, will feel ill at ease and their effectiveness will be reduced. This implies that a new style of managing is unlikely to be introduced overnight with any success.

The manager who questions his present practice might start by devoting more time to listening. If interviews are rushed he will impose rather than receive ideas. If he gives instructions as opposed to coming to a joint decision after careful evaluation of the facts and examination of alternative courses of action, then again his views will prevail. Perhaps his views are sufficiently good, but can he be sure that what he wants will be translated into action with understanding and enthusiasm? How often do managers say "I cannot rely on what I want being carried out in the way I want it done".

The way to be sure is to make the time to ensure that one's subordinates really understand what you want—not to assume that they know.

The style of a successful coach

Robert E Tannehill [2] has written:

> Coaching goes on while the subordinate is actually working on real projects connected with his work. Even if the superior manager were never to discuss performance at all with subordinates, there would still be much learning going on . . . Through skilful effective coaching, the superior manager can see to it that the subordinate's experience is shaped and directed toward a more fruitful, effective development of his strong points.

But skilful effective coaching is as much an attitude of mind as it is the expression in practice of learned techniques. The style of an effective coach will vary in detail depending on a man's personality. However, all the effective coaches in my experience have exhibited three important qualities.

They are relaxed

Even under severe pressures successful coaches manage to give the whole of their attention to their subordinates' problems and ideas. They recognize that the time spent is actually working on real projects and not an added extra to be fitted into an overcrowded schedule. Instinctively they appear to recognize that time spent on coaching, in the context of the everyday life of the organization, is creating a time bonus at a later date by the avoidance of the need for a clearing up operation. The good coach is, therefore, selective in his choice of topics on which to coach. He knows that success lies in a joint recognition that the time spent will be productive in furthering a solution to a known problem.

They recognize the importance of people

Good coaches know that results are achieved mainly by people and not solely by adherence to a system. They understand that a system can be an aid to, not a substitute for, effective decision making by an individual. They recognize, therefore, that time spent on people is more important than time spent on things. If men are helped to develop then the decisions which need to be made will follow. If a manager has six subordinates he is offered the choice either to make most of the decisions himself and hope that his people will carry them out effectively, or to take the opportunity to develop six men to think for themselves so that they have the confidence to make their own effective decisions. A little thought may well lead to the conclusion that fewer decisions made by a manager can easily lead to more decisive management by the team of seven men, provided that the leader of the team devotes a major part of the time he saves through making fewer decisions to helping and guiding his subordinates to develop their own skills.

They recognize that a large part of a manager's job is leading and co-ordinating the work of others

It is axiomatic to talk of a manager as a leader and a co-ordinator. It is strange how often managers lead by direction and co-ordinate by dictation. Such practices result inevitably in a loss of initiative at lower levels and a loss of a sense of personal responsibility for results. If the 'old man' is taking all the worthwhile decisions there is little incentive left to experiment or to innovate. More serious is the loss of job interest and the feeling of frustration when things go wrong. Lower levels of management, faced with seemingly intractable problems of which they are fully aware, take refuge from shouldering personal responsibility for events by blaming the system.

In an engineering company foremen were faced with production planning problems accentuated by indifferent labour relations, or as they expressed it 'lack of shop floor discipline.' They readily blamed the planning system and the personnel department for their problems. The former was inadequate for their needs, while the personnel department was seen as abrogating its authority. It can be admitted that both these could have been contributory factors to an unsatisfactory situation, but was there really any excuse for foremen who allowed men to clock-off early, fiddle their piece-work earnings or leave their job for excessive rest breaks? Discussions with the foremen showed that their own deteriorating morale stemmed from a management who appeared to leave all the unpleasant tasks to the foremen and failed to provide an adequate solution to the more interesting aspects of shop floor production. There were the usual charges that senior management did not support the foremen when they tried to impose discipline.

In this unfortunately common situation senior management cannot afford not to re-examine its own attitudes and to question the wider aspects of decision making. Apart from the obvious merits of increasing job interest and utilizing the skills and experience of those nearest the shop floor in the process of decision making, is it fair to make decisions which patently are unsatisfactory and then blame those who carry out the decisions for not making them work satisfactorily?

If senior management is up to its job it should be able to guide and to coach subordinates to contribute to, and to understand, the reasons for a particular policy. If the coaching is well conducted the coach will learn, and the subordinates will know that they have made a positive contribution. When a man feels involved it is surprising how often he will find a means of achieving desired results. Leading and co-ordinating the work of others, therefore, means coaching, guiding, and involving subordinates rather than giving instructions.

1 Riegel J W, *Executive Development Bureau of Industrial Relations,* Report No 5
2 Tannehill Robert E, *Motivation and Management Development*, Butterworths, 1970

CHAPTER 5

How do people learn?

This is not a chapter on learning theory, but rather some introductory remarks which, it is hoped, will place the next two chapters, on the skills of coaching, in perspective. These skills are a means to an end which in this case is to help individuals to learn. The skills have many applications such as selecting applicants for jobs, reviewing performance, acting as a chairman and so on. But they are of little use in isolation. So we introduce them by thinking about their relevance in the learning process.

In the world of industry and commerce we pay people to think, not to act as automatons. If there are lingering doubts about this the impact of microprocessors and increased automation will remove them. To think about something is to learn, so one of the most important facets of creating a situation in which a person is encouraged to learn is to ensure that he is encouraged to think—to use his brains.

Consider the ingredients of thinking more closely. One can only think when one has knowledge, but equally one can only apply knowledge when one has applied thought. The result of applied thinking is to create some kind of experience or action. To learn is to discover whether the action we took turned out as we expected, which creates new knowledge.

The circle then begins again which we can express diagramatically:

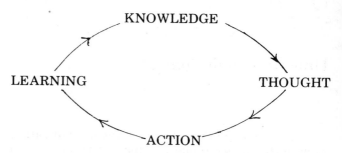

There are thus close ties between knowledge, thought and performance; the coaching process is concerned with helping someone to acquire knowledge and apply thought to what he has learned.

In the context of industry and commerce there are two types of knowledge:

conceptual knowledge, eg planning systems, cost control systems etc . . .

specific job knowledge, eg the prices charged for a product, quality standards etc . . .

and the coach needs to ensure that his people have sufficient of each type to be able to undertake their task responsibilities adequately.

Here we encounter another difficulty. Most people will only acquire knowledge, ie learn, when they feel a need to do so. It is no use saying to someone 'You ought to learn about . . .' unless you can also convince him of the relevance of his making the effort. The good coach will therefore take steps to help people to understand why they need to learn.

To summarize, people learn as a result of applying thought to knowledge and taking some kind of action. But they will only be willing to acquire knowledge if they see its relevance to their work tasks. Thus people learn by thinking and doing and this has profound implications for the coaching process.

In the previous chapter we recognized the importance of encouraging subordinates to think for themselves, and not to rely on their bosses to do their thinking for them. This means that a large part of a coaching discussion will be taken up by the person being coached doing the talking—not by the coach uttering words of wisdom. This is the coaching manifestation of the principle that people learn by doing. In this context the 'doing' is talking—as opposed to the more passive activity of listening.

This is why lecturing is such a poor medium for teaching. Think about how much you really remembered and learned as a result of a lecture which you have attended. You may have enjoyed the experience for its entertainment value. You will have evaluated the speaker's thoughts against your own experiences or prejudices. But how much of substance did you remember—how much did you really learn?

I believe that the person who learns most from giving a lecture is the speaker. As he talks he develops his own thinking and learns from it. So the good coach encourages his subordinate to do most of the talking because he knows that through talking the individual will learn. However, the talking must be to some purpose, so the skilful coach asks questions which will help the subordinate to structure his talking and therefore his thinking.

As an individual talks so he will recognize that there may be knowledge which he has not yet acquired. He will therefore either seek to acquire it, or be willing to learn or to 'listen' to what he is told.

The general structure of a coaching session, however short, is therefore likely to be:

asking a question to encourage the individual to think

asking further questions which will stimulate his thinking

supplying information which satisfies the individual's need for knowledge

encouraging the individual to use this new knowledge in order to develop his thinking

agreeing some kind of action which will translate what has been learned into action.

Diagramatically the process looks likes this:

Coach	Individual
Asks questions	Talks and thinks
Stimulates thinking	Talks, thinks and recognizes need for further knowledge
Supplies further knowledge	Thinks and talks and develops programme of action
Agrees action and summarizes	

This diagram is a gross over-simplification because it assumes that all the thinking is being done by the individual and that the coach supplies all the knowledge. In reality, as all good teachers know, they will learn from their 'pupils'. Thus the coach will also acquire knowledge and talk, think and develop programmes of action. Any coaching session is therefore a two way learning process, but because of his greater knowledge and experience the coach must take the lead by stimulating thought by the person being coached. Which means that good coaching practice is less about 'telling' someone, and more about helping them to think constructively.

So we have discovered that people learn by thinking and by taking action. There is, however, a further stage in the process of learning. As Sir Frederic Bartlett wrote in 1947: [1]

> The old saying that practice makes perfect is not true. But it is true to say that it is practice, *the results of which are known*, which makes perfect.

It is also true that the shorter the time interval between taking action and knowing about the results of that action, the greater will be the learning. In the context of industrial coaching it is therefore important for the coach to encourage the subordinate to think how he will know whether his actions are successful. This has implications for the provision of control data. In principle it is better to encourage a system of 'self-control' than one where the subordinate only hears whether he has been successful from his manager. Systems of self-control encourage a man to stand on his own feet, and to take corrective action at the earliest opportunity. The question "How will you know if this action is successful?" can stimulate thought about 'knowing about results'.

We can now examine in detail some of the skills which successful coaches have learned which enable them to put into practice the concepts outlined in this chapter.

---

1 BARTLETT, SIR FREDERIC, 'The Measurement of Human Skills', *British Medical Journal*, Vol 1, p 835, 1947

CHAPTER 6

The skills of coaching: observation, listening and appraisal

As in other fields of human activity, a learner has to start somewhere; he must learn the basic skills in whatever he undertakes. The successful coach, like the successful manager, does not behave in a stereotyped manner. As he gains proficiency he develops a style suitable to his temperament and abilities. This is the way in which a good player learns the basic skills of the game as, for example, in acquiring a smooth golf swing or keeping bat and pad in line with the ball. The individual style of his play comes later. Successful unorthodoxy is the superimposition of individual style on sound basic skills. This and the next chapter examine some of the basic skills required if success is to be attained in coaching. It is accepted that experienced practitioners will use them in a way which blends the 'orthodox' with the day to day modifications required by the time pressures to which they are subjected.

The manager who wishes to develop his own skills in coaching is likely, however, to make a conscious effort to acquire the skills before he can afford the luxury of using them as 'second nature' to his style of managing. Initially, therefore, he will need to budget time to practise. The skills we examine can be termed, *observation, listening, appraisal, discussion* and *delegation*.

Observation

This is the ability to seize opportunities to help one's subordinates to develop. In any work situation a manager deals constantly with a stream of new enquiries or tasks. He will deal with most of these himself, and will often, as a result, complain of being overworked. The good coach, however, will be aware that some of these enquiries or tasks provide opportunities for his subordinates to learn. Initially, of course, it may be time consuming to explain what is required and to give the help and guidance required, but in the longer term the manager will find that he has hit upon a way of easing his load whilst, at the same time, increasing the skills and abilities of those below him. Observation, therefore, is looking critically at one's own work, and asking whether some of it could be done by a subordinate as part of his general development. Observation above all demands of a manager sufficient humility to know that people below him are also capable of performing well, and giving them the opportunity to demonstrate his faith in them.

Listening

Because of our capacity to hear and to think at the same time listening is one of the more difficult skills to acquire. If we are honest most of us listen to what a man is saying and think about our reply—about the arguments we intend to deploy in rebuttal of what has been said. Listening, in the sense the word is used here means not only hearing what is being said, but also attempting to understand what lies behind the words spoken. It also implies a capacity to hear, and to interpret accurately, these words. Too often we dispute on the basis of what we thought a man said, rather than on what he actually said.

The good listener recognizes that the other person has something constructive to offer and seeks to discover what this is, even though the thoughts may be expressed badly. Only if a coach can understand his pupil's thoughts will he be able to influence his thinking in a desired direction. Listening, then, is the starting point for coaching, because by listening the coach establishes the point to which the student's thoughts have developed and from which further progress can be made.

The spoken word is by definition fleeting. The listener unlike the reader, cannot afford to let his attention wander even momentarily. The reader can set aside his book and resume later, whenever he pleases. The listener has a more difficult problem. He cannot, if he is to get the message, stop listening even for a short while, for the spoken word dies the moment it leaves the speaker's lips. Job, as the Bible records, recognized this problem in reverse as a speaker: "Oh that my words were now written! Oh that they were printed in a book." The listener has only one means of recalling what he has missed and that is to ask the speaker to repeat his words. We are seldom willing to do this because it draws attention to the fact that we ourselves have been inattentive.

The difference between hearing and listening

Hearing and listening are not the same thing. We hear much to which we do not listen and often we are aware of a sound only after it has ceased. Listening involves attending to the sound, identifying it correctly, and attaching the correct meaning to it. Hear-

70

ing, therefore, is only the first step in the complete process of listening effectively. There are four levels of listening skill, each one being progressively more difficult to acquire:

1 The listener must be able to hear the words clearly. This may be frustrated by the speaker mumbling, or a high level of background noise.

2 The listener must be able to identify the language being used. Language encompasses not only English, French, German, and so on, but the use of technical words, or jargon, which may mean one thing to the speaker and another to the listener. To understand words is not as simple as it sounds. The listener must try to understand the word in the same way as the speaker intends it to be interpreted. The size of the problem is demonstrated by the fact that the 500 most commonly used words in the English language have 10,070 dictionary definitions.

Take for example the word 'word'. Used as a noun it has seven major definitions in the Concise Oxford Dictionary:

> any sound or combination of sounds recognized as a part of speech, conveying an idea or alternative ideas . . .
> speech
> thing said, saying, remark
> news, intelligence, a message
> one's promise, assurance or responsible statement
> command, order, password, motto the Word of God.

and as a verb it means:

> put into words, phrase, select words, to express

3 The listener must be able to discriminate between fact and fancy in what the speaker is saying:

I'll have a design out for that by coffee break

Everyone in this plant should be paid at least the average. (This is a true statement from a negotiation session!)

I'll only be a minute, darling. (Every man has his own interpretation of this statement, and wives react in a similar way when they hear their husbands give the same response when called to a meal!)

This skill is normally acquired by experience of the speaker's previous behaviour.

4 The listener must be able to put himself in the speaker's position so that he can see the subject from the speaker's viewpoint. Many people are reluctant to adopt this position because it may require them to change their attitude to the subject under discussion. This is the most difficult of the four skills to master. All of us have time to think while we are listening. Most of us use this time to consider the next statement we shall make when the speaker has stopped or paused for breath. The effective coach tries to understand what lies behind the subordinate's words. Why is he saying what he is? Only by understanding words from the subordinate's viewpoint can a coach phrase his next question, or statement, in a way which will help the subordinate to learn.

Effective listening requires a continuous determined effort to pay attention to the speaker and to his words. It requires considerable mental effort, not only to comprehend but also to sift his statements and to store some of his points for future use. It is tiring and the manager who attempts conscientiously to listen well will know that he has succeeded when he recognizes the considerable effort he has put into his passive role in the discussion. A good listener also requires the humility to ask for further explanation of points which he does not understand fully.

Why is it difficult to listen well?

Most people find it difficult to listen well for one or more of the following reasons:

There may be something unusual or irritating about the speaker's appearance, voice, accent, pronunciation or manner. The coach should know his people sufficiently well to be able to overcome these obstacles.

We think about four to five times as fast as we speak. Thus, when somebody else is speaking our minds have much free time to wander away from the speaker. This time could be used to comprehend what lies behind the speaker's words.

We are normally more concerned with our own thoughts and generally find it more pleasant and easier to pursue these rather than to exert ourselves to follow what somebody else is saying.

We have all taught ourselves from an early age to listen to many things at the same time whilst paying the minimum amount of attention required to 'understand' anyone. We have to do this because our ears are assailed continually by a wide variety of sounds. To attempt to listen attentively to all the sounds we hear would be an impossible task so we train ourselves to pick out here and there sounds which interest us most at any moment. This habit, which we all have, of switching our listening from one thing to another, makes it difficult for us to pay attention to any one thing for a protracted period. In a coaching situation the danger lies in the possibility that, unless we pay continuous positive attention, we hear only those things which confirm our existing prejudices. Also information, unless it is particularly stressed by the speaker, may pass unnoticed. We cannot rely on the speaker to stress these points for he may feel that they are commonplace or obvious, and be unaware of their possible greater significance to his audience.

What the other man says may evoke a reply from us. If it does, instead of listening to the remainder of what he says we occupy our minds composing a devastating comment or a question in reply.

These are difficult barriers to overcome. An awareness that they exist, and constant practice in attempting to minimize their effect on our listening ability, will improve our skill in this vital aspect of coaching.

Some guidelines to effective listening

A coach can take into consideration a number of points which will improve his chances of listening well. Many of them should be obvious but are worth listing simply because they are overlooked so often in the day to day routine of a manager's life.

Coaching should preferably be carried out under the correct physical conditions. A quiet office, secure from interruptions (particularly the telephone) provides the ideal setting. However, as any encounter with a subordinate offers an opportunity for coaching ideal settings will not always be available. The good coach will be aware that he may be easily distracted and take extra care to listen to what is being said to him.

Nor should the coach be tired, for listening is itself

fatiguing—so try to avoid coaching at the end of the working day. The manager should be aware of his own mental barriers to listening well. We can assume that he will never be indifferent to what his subordinate says, but he may have so prejudiced a view of the subject matter that he may close his mind to what *is* being said. Alternatively, instead of listening with the objective of learning, he may listen merely to find flaws in the speaker's case. So try to coach when you are not particularly irritated with the subordinate because you are likely to spend more time justifying your irritation than in listening to what he has to say.

The next tip is difficult to heed because we are all subject to our prejudices and experiences. Many of us react automatically to certain words that have an unhappy or unfavourable connotation for us. Words like communist, income-tax, hippie, mother-in-law, shop-steward, capitalists and so on may cause us to react emotionally and to develop thoughts which prevent us from paying full attention to the speaker. So when your subordinate uses a word or phrase which annoys you try consciously to pay particular attention to his next sentence. Sometimes you may find the strain of listening lessens your ability to understand the speaker. His material may be difficult to follow, or his thoughts confused. If he loses you, ask a question to clarify your own thinking or understanding. It is better to interrupt in this way than to become a prey to thoughts about the inability of the speaker to present any of his thoughts in a coherent manner.

Look at your subordinate while he is talking. This is more than a matter of good manners because speakers use gestures and facial expressions to reinforce their words. It is interesting to note that the demeanour of a witness in court is accepted as 'real evidence'. C F Cross writes in *Evidence,* "If a witness gives his evidence in a forthright way, unperturbed by cross-examination, the court will no doubt be more disposed to believe him than would be the case with a halting or prevaricating witness." The listener who does not look at a speaker may not receive the complete message.

When we know a man well it is easy to pre-judge what he is going to say and to decide in advance that his words will contain nothing new of value. Most of us are well aware when this is happening. It is worth making a conscious effort to understand why he is re-stating a position which is already well-known to us. To do so is, at least, more constructive than thinking what we are going to say to rebut his statement. It is worth remembering that our likely rebuttal will be well known to him already. If we are not careful the conversation is likely to degenerate into an adult version of children's *Yes, you did, No, I didn't, Yes, you did* etc type of exchange.

Guard particularly against the temptation to simulate attention when privately pursuing your own thoughts. Most people doing this do not succeed in deceiving the speaker, because paying attention produces some response in the eyes lacking if one's thoughts are elsewhere.

Plan your listening

To listen effectively requires us to develop a pattern of

listen
review
think.

Listen for the speaker's main points. You cannot hope to remember everything that is said. You can make a conscious attempt to isolate the main point of what you hear by taking a written note of each main point as it occurs to you.

Review regularly what the speaker has said so far. You may wish to do this verbally as suggested in the next chapter under the heading *Discussion*.

Think ahead to anticipate the speaker's next point. If you guess correctly you increase the chances of remembering the point afterwards. If you are wrong compare your point with the point you hear. The principle of comparing and contrasting is well known as a means of learning. Don't, however, just assume what the speaker's next point is going to be and 'switch off'. Keep an open mind even as you seek to anticipate the subordinate's next opinion. He may make a statement that could change your assessment of the situation.

Listening with understanding

A coach must combine understanding with listening. The subordinate's feelings are as important as his words. His feelings may be gauged by his physical expressions. the way he phrases his thoughts, or his reluctance or readiness to discuss a point. It is by no means easy to listen to interpret feelings, but if the coach is successful he will pick up important clues as to the best way to steer the conversation.

The ability to listen well is perhaps the most important of the skills possessed by a coach for it demonstrates to the subordinate that his superior manager is not only taking an interest but feels that the subordinate has something worthwhile to say. This is a sure foundation upon which to build.

Appraisal

The use of the word 'appraisal' is a fine example of the

misunderstanding which can arise through the use of a word having several meanings. You will be thinking probably in terms of performance appraisal, which is discussed in a later chapter. In the context of coaching skills 'appraisal' means the ability to assess how much new learning the subordinate has acquired during the coaching session. Not only what has been learned, but also whether the man has understood the requirement for the acquisition of new knowledge.

This is not a straightforward matter because the coach can confuse ready agreement by the subordinate with acceptance or understanding. Most people prefer, or find it easier, to agree with a speaker, unless it is a matter which they regard as important. This is particularly the case in conversations with a superior. Ask yourself whether you tend to agree most of the time with your superior, or at least to give him the benefit of the doubt if his statement strikes you as ambiguous. If you don't believe this, test it out next time you talk to your boss about work. It would be strange, and unnatural, if subordinates disagreed constantly with their bosses. Most of us would wonder how long we could remain that man's subordinate. So for reasons of self preservation we tend to agree rather than to disagree with our superiors.

In a coaching situation the manager needs to be well aware of this tendency to agree. He is required to test his subordinate's understanding of points. This can be done by putting further questions (not capable of being answered by simple assent or dissent) and by steering the conversation in a way which reveals whether the subordinate has really understood the point under discussion. Try, above all, to avoid asking 'Do you understand that?' Nine times out of 10 it will bring a positive response.

Because of this danger of passive concurrence further feed-back can be gained by telling your subordinate what you understand by what he is saying, or by letting him know your interpretation of his words. This leaves it open for him:

to agree with you in a truthful and confident manner

to agree, but untruthfully. In this case he may think he is being tactful

to put you right.

You may be able to determine which of the first two responses you are receiving by his facial, or other, expressions.

Occasionally understanding can be tested by asking the subordinate to make notes of important aspects of a coaching session 'for the record'. This will give a delayed feed-back on the degree of acceptance and understanding of the items covered.

CHAPTER 7

The skills of coaching: discussion and delegation

The ideal coaching session is between equals, not between supervisor and subordinate. This must be made apparent to the subordinate. He is unlikely to believe it unless the supervisor, by his attitude and actions over a period, engenders in the subordinate the feeling that his manager has a sincere desire to reveal all relevant facts and opinions. The role of the supervisor is to help his subordinate to learn; he will achieve this by bringing to bear his greater experience and wider view of problems.

Discussion

Discussion is concerned with the diagnosis and the solution of work problems. It should not be the issuing of instructions or the imposing of solutions. Because of the hierarchical and autocratic nature of our industrial society good coaches have to be particularly careful not to give the impression of imposing a solution. There are many instances of a manager putting forward an idea for discussion, only to find that his subordinates assume that the idea is to be acted upon. I know of one case where a managing director idly put forward an idea for a modification to a product only to find, to his astonishment and horror, that many hours and considerable sums of money were then spent in trying, unsuccessfully, to make the idea work!

Many good coaches, therefore, conceal their own thoughts until later in the discussion, in order not to over-influence the thinking of their subordinates. Rather than appearing to act as judge and sole arbiter regarding their subordinates' actions, they encourage them to provide answers to their problems by careful questioning and commenting. A manager can help in a discussion by providing questions suitably phrased to highlight weak or illogical areas, at the same time leaving subordinates to discuss and to correct their own errors in thinking. In this way the chances are increased that they will not feel that they have to justify their actions to a boss, but will be willing to sit down on a 'person to person' basis to discuss freely the problems that affect them.

A readiness to admit one's own responsibility for mistakes is another means of convincing subordinates that a discussion of a problem is not an occasion for issuing orders. The phrase 'Can you help me', sincerely meant, is one useful method of initiating a problem solving and coaching session.

Some points to remember

A coach is interested in what his subordinates really think—not in what they think he wants to hear. Only in this way can he be of help to them. His task is to analyse their learning needs and to assist them in their acquisition of knowledge and understanding. The following are some ideas to bear in mind which will open up, rather than inhibit, discussion:

Refrain from making statements, or asking questions, which may make the subordinate think that you are judging him. 'Let's see how that will work' is a better phrase than 'I don't think that way would work'.

Let the man put forward all his ideas. You can easily stifle 'winners' by dismissing some out of hand. One good idea out of 10 discussed is a respectable score. Do you do better?

Try to put yourself in his shoes so as to understand his ideas and feelings. If you're trying to coach for the first time he may wish to get a lot off his chest. Who knows he may feel it's his only chance?

Ensure that you understand what he is really trying to say. Poor communication can be a prime cause of misunderstanding and everyone isn't as good as you think in giving expression to their thoughts.

Try not to put him on the spot by exposing his weaknesses. This may be good for your ego but will put him on the defensive and so reduce his willingness to contribute freely. What would happen if he felt free to expose your weaknesses?

Encourage him to develop his own thinking. By all means give him any necessary information, but try not to take short cuts and provide the answers.

The coach has the responsibility for helping to structure the discussion so that it covers problem areas and leads to action, but he must not prevent the subordinate from raising matters which he feels to be important. A discussion can be structured in the following way:

Begin by explaining the object of the discussion. Alternatively the subordinate may on occasion precipitate the discussion with a problem, in which case the coach should show that he is willing to help, but also indicate that the solution will be a joint one.

If the problem is not clearly defined the first step is for both men to talk around the subject and to isolate and to state the problem clearly. Fifty per cent of successful coaching depends on isolating the correct problem. So often the apparent difficulty is only a manifestation of some more fundamental or deep seated matter requiring exploration and discussion. Managers, no doubt because of time pressures, seem to over simplify problems and look for instant solutions, when a little thought would lead them in the right direction. To help them to do this is a major objective of coaching. The difficulty lies partly in a lack of system in analysing non-technical matters, but there is a tendency to try to solve non-technical aspects by intuition.

When the correct problem has been isolated encourage the subordinate to suggest as many solutions as possible. Many men can see only one solution to a problem. Helping them to develop alternative strategies is a major coaching success.

By questioning, and where necessary providing information, the coach can assist the man to evaluate his suggested solutions and to choose one as a basis for action.

Finally the coach should discuss the subordinate's plan in some detail and then give him responsibility for carrying it out. Remember that people learn more by doing than by talking about what should be done.

During the whole of the discussion the coach will keep encouraging the subordinate to think through the problem. He will provide any inputs of information required. This provides an opportunity to enlarge the man's knowledge. However, be careful not to confuse supplying factual information with imposing a solution.

Skill is needed to discuss well

A successful coaching discussion depends on many factors, not least the nature of the relationship between the subordinate and his manager. A man will find it difficult to learn from someone for whom he does not have respect. Similarly he will be suspicious if his superior does not normally use a style of management which is to some degree participative. A manager who tries to be participative when he is in a coaching situation but appears to be overly autocratic at other times is unlikely to appear credible during a coaching session. His subordinate will remember his more usual behaviour and react accordingly. We all look for consistency in our relationships with others.

Bearing these limitations in mind there are, however, a number of discussion skills which the would-be coach must understand and master:

Listening

We have referred to this skill in the previous chapter. All we require to add in the context of holding a discussion is that the manager must listen well if the subordinate is not to be discouraged from participating. Many good coaches state that they find that they are listening for three-quarters of a good discussion. Often the purpose of a coaching discussion is to help the subordinate to identify areas where he requires more knowledge. When these areas have been isolated he may then in turn listen to his coach; but at this stage the original discussion has ended and the coach is supplying inputs of information and knowledge.

Use of pauses

Discussions which are intended to solve problems (and most discussions at work are of this kind) inevitably require the subordinate to think. He cannot, or at least should not, pour out ideas without prior thought as to their relevance. If he does we are in a 'brainstorming' situation and this is another subject altogether. Thus, when a subordinate stops talking the manager should not feel that it is his duty immediately to take up the conversation again. It is often more rewarding to allow a pause which encourages the subordinate to expand the point, and to bring up facts or views which would otherwise have not been expressed. The use of a facial expression of encouragement for a subordinate to continue in his own time may be all that is required.

To discipline oneself to say nothing is difficult. We all hate a vacuum in a conversation. Somehow silence seems threatening and appears to last a long time. Next time you hold a conversation try to impose a five second pause. It will seem an age. Conversely, consider how little one really says in 10 seconds and how quickly the time passes.

Spotting and understanding the feelings of the subordinate

Subordinates express their true feelings either explicitly by making statements or, more often, implicitly by their behaviour, facial expressions or by the way they phrase or express their statements. The coach needs to identify and to respond to such feelings. It is important for him to persuade the

85

subordinate to state his feelings explicitly for only then can they be analysed and dealt with. The subordinate may feel uneasy about his own performance, the performance of others, or the work situation in general. If he can be persuaded to express these feelings then the two men, together, can discuss a plan for action to overcome the problems caused by the situation. The feelings of a subordinate may be based on emotional factors. A major role of the coach is to help to remove the emotion and to assist the man to consider the facts of the situation in a calmer manner. One way of doing this is to reflect the subordinate's feelings and so allow the subordinate to examine why he feels the way he does. Consider these two examples, one explicit and one implicit.

Explicit

It is the beginning of a discussion about the month's results.

Sub   *What a morning! Never a moment's peace and I always like 10 minutes or so before one of these discussions to get myself in the right frame of mind.*

Coach   *Why do you need 10 minutes?*

Implicit

During the same discussion.

Sub   *No, I don't think I'll give the job to Bill, I'll do it myself.*

Coach   *That's interesting—I wonder why you think Bill can't do this work.*

In the first example the subordinate has said that he needs to approach the discussion in the right frame of mind. The coach has reflected this feeling of agitation and asked an indirect question which he hopes will enable the subordinate to be more explicit about the reasons why he feels disturbed.

In the second the subordinate has made no explicit comment about Bill's ability, yet some feeling on his part about it is implied. The coach has noticed this and has asked a question which will enable the subordinate to express his feelings explicitly.

Coaches should, however, be aware of two points when reflecting feelings:

constantly reflecting feelings, some of which may not concern the job, may put the subordinate on the defensive and he may refuse to explain them

reflecting 'touchy' points, which may be personal ones, is likely to do more harm than good. The coach's sole concern should be to assist the subordinate in matters related to his job.

Reflecting feelings must be done with caution, but it is often a useful means of helping a subordinate to express his true opinions should he wish to do so. Certainly it is a better way of developing a discussion than the following kinds of reaction as applied to the examples above:

Example 1
Coach   No response, or
        Yes, I'm a busy man as well.
Example 2
Coach   I agree, Bill made a hell of a mess of it last
        time.

Summarizing

A useful skill, when applied at the correct time, is for the coach to summarize what has been said in his own words. Summaries may be used to:

recapitulate on what has been covered and show
how it fits into an overall pattern

show that the coach understands what has been
said and is aware of the feelings expressed

show what problems have been covered and what
still remain to be resolved

help the subordinate to sort out the areas of
his own thinking which may have been
confused.

Some examples of when it may be appropriate to
summarize are:

when the discussion has become bogged down in
trivia

when the subordinate is not contributing sufficiently

when a large amount of ground has been covered

when the coach feels that either he or the subordinate is lost and that they do not understand one
another.

Often a good summary can lead to either man
taking a note which will be used later as a basis for
action.

The ability to summarize is one of the key skills in
successful coaching. Certainly it helps the coach to
keep control of the discussion without appearing to do
so. Although it is easy to summarize, particularly if
one has been taking notes, people seem to feel awkward about summarizing. If you persevere you will
find that there is no awkwardness—rather the
reverse in that the other person will appreciate your
ability to help to keep the discussion on course. A
further advantage is that when making a summary
one often thinks of the next appropriate question to
ask, particularly when the conversation seems to be
going round in circles.

Questioning

A well framed question which can direct the subordinate's thoughts into productive channels will often make a major contribution to a well conducted discussion. Questions have varied degrees of structure. A highly structured question such as "is our product good?" invites a simple answer yes or no. A less structured question would be "What do you think of our product compared with those of our competitors?" Less structured questions require more complex and reasoned answers. The amount of response required to a question is indicated by the degree of structure.

Lowly structured questions are the best means of obtaining all the information pertinent to the point under discussion. They will elicit not only facts but also opinions and feelings, for they encourage the subordinate to expand on the subject. Four possible ways of asking lowly structured questions are:

1 Ask questions that require an explanation. Such questions are often prefaced by *how* or *what*. Conversely the prefaces *when* or *where* tend to give a question a high structure.

   How does Mr X plan his call schedule? (low structure)

   When and where does Mr X call on his customer? (high structure)

2 Preface key words from what the subordinate has said by

   What about or *How about*:

   What about the quality of the raw materials? When the subordinate has said as part of a longer statement about his production difficulties *"You know the problems we are having with labour, inspectors and the raw material we get."*

   A highly structured question would be:

Is the raw material still poor in spite of all we've done?

3 Repeat the key word in a questioning voice:
   Raw material?

4 Summarize back. By doing this the subordinate may feel it is necessary to explain further:
   What you're saying is that in spite of all we've done the raw material position hasn't improved?

   This is a highly structured question and should it only elicit the response *No* a follow up would be:
   What do you suggest we should do then?

In a coaching situation it is often, though not always, desirable to start the discussion with lowly structured questions which will require the other person to give the maximun amount of information. As the problem becomes clear more highly structured or leading questions may direct his thinking into constructive channels.

But there can be no rigid rules. The coach must be aware of what is happening and deploy his skills in the appropriate way. Just as the expert sportsman uses his highly developed skills in the order determined by events, so the expert coach needs to be aware of why he is using a particular skill at a certain point in the conversation. Only conscious and regular practice will lead to successful performance on the part of both sportsman and coach.

Delegation

One of the results of coaching should be that the subordinate is able, and willing, to shoulder increased responsibilities. To delegate well requires skill on the part of the manager—it should be much more than saying to a man 'I want you to take responsibility for this.' The act of delegation implies:

the transfer of initiative, responsibility and authority to another for the performance of agreed tasks

the retention by the delegator of the means of exercising overall control and for checking the performance of the subordinate

the willingness of the delegator to delegate and the willingness of the subordinate to accept responsibility for the tasks assigned.

Thus delegation requires three actions: the assignment of tasks, the granting of authority and the assumption of responsibility by the subordinate. This means that every subordinate's job description is a summary of tasks delegated to him and that delegation is not just assigning additional tasks on a short term basis.

When assigning new tasks both the manager and the subordinate need to be clear about what tasks have been delegated. This requires discussion between them. It should be insufficient for them to agree that the subordinate's responsibility is, for example, 'To improve our sales to African countries.' A better responsibility is, 'To increase our sales to our customers in Africa by two per cent in the next six months.'

Notice that the latter responsibility, being more explicit, allows both men to measure how well the delegated task has been performed. It allows the subordinate as much freedom of action as the more loosely worded responsibility. This stricter definition of the responsibility may well avoid misunderstanding later as to exactly what was delegated. It has the added advantage of making the task more interesting to the subordinate. He has a target to achieve—a definite goal for which to strive. It is not much fun playing darts on a dartboard which has no numbers. Similarly, real learning only takes place when there can be a feed back of information. To the proposition 'improve our sales' an alert subordinate should wonder 'by how much?' and 'by when?' Many of the problems encountered in delegation stem from the fact that managers have failed to define the precise nature of the task delegated.

When granting authority to undertake new tasks a manager should be aware that he can grant authority only to the limit that it is vested in him and within the policies of the organization. Thus a manager cannot grant a subordinate the authority to hire and fire if he himself does not have that authority. Should he be able to delegate powers of recruitment and dismissal such powers (and authority) will still be restricted to observance of company procedures, manpower budgets and so on.

For example, a manager may delegate authority to dismiss a man for say persistent bad time keeping. However, there may be a company wide definition of what constitutes bad time keeping, and there will almost certainly be a system of prior warnings which must be strictly adhered to before dismissal takes place.

Even the simplest granting of authority is likely to be subject to limitations. Unless both the manager and his subordinate are aware of these limitations, and of any increase in the complexity of the delegated task which arises from them, the act of delegation may well lead to inadequate performance by the subordinate.

This is why coaching is so important in the process of delegation. By their very nature the delegated tasks are likely to be novel to the subordinate. Before delegating, the manager needs to consider what new knowledge (and skills) the subordinate will require in order to perform well. These matters should become then the subject of discussion and coaching between the two men.

A simple means of entering into this phase of the discussion is to ask "How will you set about this task?"

Some guide rules for good delegation

The following are some of the points to bear in mind before delegating new tasks to a subordinate:

1 Agree with him the work for which you will hold him accountable.
2 Put this information on paper—not only in a job definition but also in any other document you may find appropriate (This avoids subsequent discussion on the lines of "I thought you understood that . . .")
3 Agree, wherever possible, to define the results that are expected.
4 Ensure that you have given the subordinate the necessary authority to take the kinds of action which are involved in carrying out the job satisfactorily.
5 Let the subordinate stand on his own feet. Allow him to get on with the job without interference, but give him any help he asks for or clearly requires.
6 Devise, if necessary, an effective control system so that the subordinate can monitor his own progress towards the agreed goals. Ensure that he sees this information before you do. When checking up on his results take action only when really necessary to avoid a serious deviation from what is acceptable. Remember that the newly delegated tasks involve learning on the part of the subordinate. He will make mistakes and if he is of the right calibre he will learn from them to take the necessary corrective action. It is much better to be able to say: "I noticed you went off the rails in March but are

taking steps to get the situation corrected by the end of April", than "Your March results were poor—you'll have to do better in April." If you don't believe this ask yourself how you would react if you were the subordinate.

The steps in delegation

The process of delegation involves a series of steps, but the way in which each step is carried out depends on many factors. Such factors are the manager's style of leadership, the type of organization, the abilities of the subordinates and the nature of the work to be delegated. If you are delegating new tasks be certain of the need to delegate and why you wish to do so. The manager has to decide that delegation is necessary, either to lessen his own workload so that he can devote time to more important matters, or to help his subordinate to develop by giving him more demanding tasks. Whatever his reasons for delegating extra work, the manager should recognize that delegation will alter to some extent the nature of his own work. Failure to realize this results in having a dog and barking yourself.

Decide whether the task is suitable for delegation. Some of a manager's work cannot be delegated to subordinates for a number of reasons which include:

the subordinate is not equipped to carry out the delegated tasks. He may require to master new knowledge or skills over a period before he can be given full responsibility with confidence

the nature of the work is unsuitable for delegation. Involvement in company secrets or personnel records may be forbidden by the company to employees below a certain grade

although the work may be suitable for delegation the subordinate already has so heavy a work load that he cannot be expected to undertake new responsibilities without first restructuring his own work

the manager cannot spare the time to coach the subordinate and to provide any necessary follow-up. In the long-term this is, of course, self-defeating. Unless the manager manages to delegate effectively he may become overwhelmed by dealing with detail.

Discuss the new tasks with the subordinate

If the subordinate is to shoulder new responsibilities willingly he should participate in the delegation process. This allows him to understand, and to help to form, the nature of the task, its objectives, the degree of authority necessary, and the possible solution to any foreseeable problems.

Some problems of delegation

As all managers know, delegation is not always successful. This is not invariably the subordinate's fault. Some of the major pitfalls are:

inadequate definition of the limits of the subordinate's authority. This can often lead to conflict within the department, or between departments, if the subordinate assumes authority which is either greater than the manager intended, or appears to be greater than others expect. Consider, for example, the problems which arise from the often ill-defined authority given to personal assistants

although the manager has delegated well and has allowed the subordinate to carry out his work

without interference, a control department, or
even the manager himself, vets the work in such
detail that much of what has been done is repeated. This not only reduces the subordinate's
responsibility but leads to an unnecessary duplication of effort

the manager is not really committed to delegation.
He may feel that he can do the job better himself,
or he has no confidence in his subordinate, or he
interferes because he has no control information
to monitor the subordinate's performance or,
perhaps, he just does not like taking chances.
This type of manager is likely to complain of
overwork or of having to deal constantly with
trivial problems or even about his subordinate's
lack of initiative. His remedy should be to undertake a critical self-examination of his own style
of management and attitudes rather than to
blame his subordinates or the organization
structure.

Conversely, delegation may fail because the subordinate is unwilling to accept additional responsibilities. Some reasons for this may be that:

he finds it easier to ask his manager than to make
decisions himself. Delegation often demands
brainwork on the part of the subordinate, an
activity he may rarely have indulged in, or does
not particularly relish. So he passes it back to the
manager

he may feel that he will be criticized for his mistakes. An extremely critical manager who does
not accept errors lightly may discourage his subordinates from accepting tasks that cannot be
guaranteed to run smoothly and be 100 per cent
successful. This type of manager should not be
confused with the one who is demanding in his

expectations but is also willing to give help and is tolerant of mistakes provided they are not repeated

the subordinate may feel that there is insufficient information or resources to do the job properly. Such a person may be a foreman who is offered sole responsibility for working out ways of improving shop production when he feels that the machinery available to him is out of date and badly maintained

the subordinate may lack self-confidence. In this situation a skilful coach will build up his confidence by assigning him to tasks of graduated difficulty

the subordinate may feel that there are no incentives to encourage him to accept increased responsibility. He is unlikely, therefore, to derive any personal satisfaction from the new tasks

the subordinate regards the new responsibilities as an imposition, rather than a collaboration or a sharing of authority. He was not asked to join in the formulation of the new responsibility. Giving responsibility as a mark of confidence in the other's ability is radically different from imposing added responsibilities on a subordinate.

What is interesting about this list of possible causes for a lack of enthusiasm for delegation on the part of the subordinate is that they are all susceptible to action by the manager. For example has he:

always made all the important decisions himself and so discouraged subordinates from thinking for themselves?

by his attitude and actions discouraged risk taking by his subordinates, so that they tend to play it safe?

delegated an impossible task to get himself off the hook?

destroyed the self-confidence of his subordinates by consistently nit picking?

failed to recognize that although men normally relish opportunities for increased responsibility, any enthusiasm has been damped down by poor pay and bad conditions of work?

taken an autocratic decision to delegate and imposed a solution on the subordinate?

If you are one of those managers who say that men won't accept responsibility these days try asking yourself some of these questions. Honest answers may surprise you.

Delegation and coaching which enables subordinates to accept new demanding responsibilities have advantages for any manager. They enable him to undertake a wider span of control; his subordinates will develop their managerial competence faster in response to the challenge of their jobs; and they will seek more on-the-job training which will contribute to their further development. But most important of all the manager himself will be in a position to achieve better results.

CHAPTER 8

Developing the skills of coaching

The skills required to be an effective coach can only be developed by practice in the day to day context of the manager's job. In this they are similar to the development of other managerial skills. Attendance at courses to learn the techniques of management is valuable, but it can never be a substitute for the experience acquired over a period by dealing with the day to day responsibilities of a manager.

It is of course possible to be a good manager without being a good coach. It is the thesis of this book that all managers could achieve better results if they developed their skills as coaches. At first the skills of coaching require to be developed consciously by a manager, and may appear to be distinct from the skills of managing. As his coaching skills improve the manager will discover that they become natural to his style of managing and are indistinguishable from his total skills as a manager. Then he will regard coaching no longer as an added extra to his job—it will have become a way of life in the same way that a professional sportsman reacts instinctively when playing a shot which he has practised painstakingly over many months. It is open to any manager, at any level, to practise coaching of staff. There are many examples of individual managers coaching and developing subordinates well, even in companies which are not distinguished by the interest in the subject exhibited by top management.

As with so much else in management the easiest way to develop an awareness of the importance of coaching within an organization is for the chief executive to be seen actively to support a style of management in which coaching plays a major part. All senior managers discuss the performance of their subordinates with the chief executive at some time or another. This is a natural part of the managing process. What is less frequent is for chief executives to ask their senior managers what steps they are taking to coach subordinates whose performance is under review.

Mr X's performance is considered in relation to the results he achieves, how he achieves them, and his potential for wider responsibility. It is at this stage that chief executives could make the greatest impact on the development of an attitude of mind which regards coaching as important throughout a company by asking: "And what steps are you taking, personally, to help this man to develop further?"

One major company uses as one criterion for the effectiveness of its coaching the percentage of jobs which it can fill by internal promotion. In four years the proportion rose from 40 per cent to 80 per cent.

The example which a chief executive sets by his personal behaviour and attitude inevitably has a major influence on the behaviour and style of his subordinates. If, in a company where regular formal performance appraisal procedures are used, one of the factors discussed is the extent and success of a manager's coaching activities, then a major step will have been taken to introduce a climate of opinion in which coaching is seen to be important. All managers tend to concentrate on those things which they think their superiors regard as important. There is the well known story of the foremen who concentrated a major part of their activities on keeping trucks within the white lines of their production departments, sometimes to the detriment of production, because their manager's first action on entering their section was to go around and try to spot any trucks out of place. Similarly, but we hope with more important results for the company, a manager who regularly raises the subject of his subordinates' coaching activities, is likely to find that their performance in this respect will improve.

It is important that the development of coaching skills go hand in hand with the development of managerial skills. Unless a manager is regarded as effective by his subordinates his advice, help and guidance will make little impact. Setting an example is one of the most important factors in coaching. The manager who encourages his subordinates to read more widely but is known never to open a book on management is hardly likely to instil a liking for the written word in others.

Good coaching practices stem primarily from the attitude of mind of the manager; from his instinctive recognition that helping to improve the abilities of his subordinates will make his own job easier. I have yet to meet a manager who does not regard the performance of his subordinates as a major factor in his own success or failure as a manager. It is easy to recognize the truth of this statement; it is much more difficult to make the time and effort required to do something about it. The average manager when asked what training has been given to, or is needed by, his subordinates tends to talk about courses. If your company has an appraisal system, and a section of the form asks you to state what training is required, when did you last enter "I intend to spend time with Mr X helping him to . . ." It is more likely that you entered "A course on . . . would be of benefit".

Unfortunately, too many managers think that sending a man on a course is all they need to do to improve his performance. Often they think that sparing him for the time required to attend a course represents a considerable sacrifice on their own part. Attendance on courses may be a valuable development experience. It can never be a substitute for well planned on-the-job coaching. Indeed, the selection of a particular course should arise naturally from the coaching which has preceded it and fit into the coaching which will follow on the man's return.

An organization which wishes to develop the skills of coaching in its managers, and a recognition by them of its importance, can take formal action to supplement the example set by senior managers. Part of this action relates to the appraisal system in use which is discussed in more detail in a later chapter.

Arrangements can also be made for managers to attend group coaching sessions to discuss the subject. I have used the title 'group coaching' instead of a training course in order to underline the importance of the teacher practising what he preaches. It would be relatively simple to lay on a course dealing with the various skills of coaching on a 'lecture and discussion' basis. Indeed this would be the quickest method of covering the subject matter. It is doubtful, however, if much impact would be made by using this approach. Far better to involve the group in a coaching session designed to enable the participants to discover for themselves the nature of the skills involved in coaching and the style of management which will best enable coaching to flourish in their particular organization.

This demands far more of the tutor, for instead of

being able to stick to a well prepared brief for the session he must be capable of identifying and meeting the needs of the group in their quest for knowledge. He must respond to the learning needs of the participants rather than impose on them his views of what they should learn. To do this well he must himself practise the major skills of coaching—the ability to listen with understanding. Anyone who has run one of these sessions will confirm that this takes much more effort and makes more demands than the more traditional methods of 'teaching'. The tutor will be expected to contribute to the discussion where the group clearly lacks knowledge or has become bogged down on an unprofitable exchange of views. Such interpolations should be used sparingly, for if used to excess the coaching becomes a lecture. The case history of Molins Ltd in chapter 13 is one example of group coaching.

The use of a coaching approach to teach coaching requires careful preparation before the group meets. People will only learn when they want to and when they recognize that what they are learning is relevant to their own jobs or interests. In a work situation few managers would welcome attending a session on coaching if they felt that the time could be spent more profitably in their own departments. Therefore such a session must be made to appear relevant to the needs of those attending. This implies that the subject under discussion should be seen by the participants to relate to their work problems. Each organization must decide for itself the appropriate medium through which coaching skills can be learned. The following are mediums which have been used, but it must be stressed that they may be inappropriate to your organization:

reviewing the effectiveness of a job appraisal system (in an engineering company)

how to improve supervisory skills (in a printing
  company)

how to improve the quality of field work (in an
  Industrial Training Board)

In each of these situations the basic problem was well
recognized by the participants. Before embarking on
these sessions on coaching all had agreed that their
ability to coach well could make a major contribution
to improving the effectiveness of their subordinates
in their jobs. They were well aware that coaching
alone could not solve the problem, but agreed that it
was worthwhile discussing the subject in detail
because improved on-the-job coaching would make a
significant contribution to the ability of their subordinates to perform well in carrying out their tasks.
The sessions on coaching were designed to answer the
following questions:

What is coaching?

Who is responsible for carrying it out?

What are the skills required to carry it out and
  what is the nature of those skills?

How can the skills be developed?

What support should the organization give in order
  that more coaching could be undertaken?

What is the effect of coaching on management
  style?

The topics covered during the sessions were many
and varied. A typical example is an analysis of the
characteristics displayed by a manager who is also a
good coach. The following are some points raised
during a three hour session by a group of five
managers:

1 A good coach ensures that his man makes the
   maximum contribution of which he is capable. In
   discussing a problem the manager should

104

encourage him to think out the solution even if that solution is clear to the manager. It takes longer but the man is likely to remember a thought which he has developed for himself and his confidence is built up as he proves himself to himself.

2   When attending meetings with his subordinate at which either his own boss, or the subordinate's juniors are present, he uses his skills to boost the man's confidence. He shows enough of himself to indicate that he sees clearly the whole framework of the subject under discussion, but he has confidence in his man to handle the detail.

3   The manager/coach always insists on a high standard of performance. He knows what is required and is not satisfied with a lesser standard. This implies that he may have to spend time with his man to help him to achieve the required results.

4   He does not try to mould his man into an image of himself. His aim is to build on the man's own characteristics, only curbing those which are unhelpful. A good coach allows his man the freedom to thrive as long as the required end results are being achieved.

5   The manager must guard against trying to improve on his man's ideas when they are likely to achieve the required result. Some managers develop a ping-pong habit. Their man has an idea which they feel they must strip, reclothe in their own words, and give back to him.

6   A good coach takes the trouble to make sure that he ascertains and grasps the real nature of the problem facing the subordinate. Only in this way can he make a worthwhile contribution to the discussion. His further questioning of the man will enhance his understanding of his

subordinate's difficulties. Unless he has this understanding he is entirely in the hands of the man, examining only those areas aired by him. With the full background the manager can probe further into the problem. This will help him as well as the subordinate.

7 A good deal of managerial coaching takes place in a situation where important changes are taking place eg the re-layout of a department, a new production control system, a change in sales strategy, the introduction of new cost control arrangements and so on. The project starts off well and everyone is enthusiastic, but in almost every case unforeseen snags are encountered, causing a lessening of commitment to the changes. The coach's job is to help his man to identify what causes the difficulties and to plan the action needed.

The participants in the discussion were able to cite examples of worthwhile projects which had been started and which had fizzled out when snags had been encountered. This, in their view, led to people saying: "We've tried all this before" when at a later date a renewed effort was made to overcome a well recognized problem.

8 The good coach often uses examples from similar situations to stimulate his man to discover solutions to his problems.

9 Nothing is more sterile than the creation of an artificial coaching situation. To be effective the coaching must relate to a real problem. One cannot say: "I think I'll devote this afternoon to coaching X and Y" unless the trouble has been taken to identify the expected results. The man should always be expected to learn something from the coaching.

10 A good manager/coach reads widely. This gives

him the opportunity to recommend books or articles to his subordinates, or to discuss with them a point he has himself read. The subject should, of course, be of interest to the subordinate. It is no use discussing a good book on marketing if the subordinate cannot recognize the relevance of the subject to his job.

11 The manager must be seen to have integrity. For example a manager and his subordinate may have a meeting with a superior manager, where the manager/coach agrees with his superior that something should be done. Afterwards he discusses with his man the way in which the superior manager has failed to grasp the realities of the situation, and that the coach only agreed to a solution to keep his superior happy. The coach and his subordinate must now discuss how to overcome the problem in a realistic way. This form of double-talk is likely to result in the loss of the subordinate's confidence in his manager/coach. He will be afraid that what is being said to him will also contain an element of double-talk.

12 A good manager is polite in his dealings with his subordinates. For example he does not expect to be interrupted by them in the middle of an important meeting; nor should he interrupt the meetings of his men with their subordinates. *The tutor was able to cite a good example of double-talk and lack of courtesy to subordinates from his own experience. He was discussing management style with a managing director of a medium sized company. "I have a policy of an ever-open door," said the managing director. By chance the door opened at this moment and in walked the works manager. "Can't you see I'm busy?" snapped the managing Director.*

13 The good manager keeps his promises. He does not say he will do something and then forget all about it. For busy managers, with poor short-term memories, it is a good idea to note promises on a piece of paper.

14 The manager/coach constantly needs to assess the effort being made by his subordinates. This normally falls into three categories:

sustained effort with good results deserves recognition

sustained effort with inadequate results requires guidance and encouragement

the man is having an easy time, is not getting results but produces many reasons for failure. This requires straightforward and firm action. Some typical ways of doing this are to review the progress made, to agree on demanding targets for achievement by given dates, and maintaining closer contact if the man concerned works largely on his own (eg a salesman).

15 Sometimes a subordinate requires help in identifying his best course of action. The coach can help him to:

identify the practical choices.

measure the relative benefits of each. (This may require additional information).

decide on which course to take

identify any additional resources required, and help him to get them.

16 A good coach often appears to have a touch of magic. He develops an ability to put his finger unerringly on the weak spot or crucial point in a piece of work. But he does this in such a way that his man is given the opportunity to appear to have thought it up for himself and to have a remedy in mind. Part of this magical quality

stems from the manager's feel for the job. He can ask himself:

has it progressed as far as he would have hoped?

what sort of problems is the man talking about? If he is only dealing with trivia something will be amiss

is his man over-elaborating the detail in his discussion? If he is there may be important gaps.

can the man sum up his progress? If not he may be floundering.

Good managers acquire this magical quality by consciously relating to their previous experiences in similar situations and by their knowledge of the people with whom they are dealing.

17 The good manager/coach is helpful, not only in what he says but in what he offers to do. We all know of people who offer 'all help short of real assistance'. The subordinate may have a heavy work load and require another 'pair of hands'. His manager should be alert for the opportunity to help and he should provide it effectively and without delay.

To summarize, this group of managers decided that the effective manager/coach exhibited a highly demanding assortment of skills and qualities. They can be categorized as follows:

he helps his men to succeed

he comprehends the needs of the situation

he ensures that the work is performed successfully

he maintains his own personal development

he upholds and requires the highest standards of personal integrity and behaviour.

All the points outlined in this case history were made and developed by the group of managers. The tutor's role was not to state the points but rather to ask lowly structured questions designed to bring out the ideas. It is interesting to note how these practical managers developed the theme stated in chapter 4 of this book, about the characteristics of good coaches. Afterwards a number of managers remarked that they had not learned anything new. What the session had achieved was to bring to the forefront of their thinking many topics which had been recognized previously only in an unorganized way. They regarded this as valuable and relevant to their jobs, as it provided them with a framework on which to build more effective habits of coaching.

Although the most effective form of training in how to coach takes place within the organization, outside courses can play their part. Many of these deal with the behavioural sciences, either exclusively or as part of a more general management course. It is to be hoped that more of these courses will deal with the subject of coaching possibly as part of the syllabus dealing with the development of the personal skills of a manager. For example, at the Urwick Management Centre some 10 hours are devoted to discussion and practice of personal skills during the six-week general management course, and the topic of coaching is raised in a number of ways.

The Irish Management Institute has offered an interesting one day seminar on coaching. The programme was as follows:

Session 1 A discussion of the elements of coaching
Session 2 A role playing exercise in 'how to coach'
Session 3 Discussion groups: "What are the barriers to effective coaching in our organizations?"
Session 4 Reporting back and general discussion of the points raised.

The follow up to this seminar showed that those

110

attending felt that it had been valuable in highlighting an important subject, but that real progress in introducing the ideas discussed could only be made after further discussion within their companies.

There is still need for more skills training on general management courses. An undue proportion of time is spent discussing what ought to be done without giving practice in developing the skills for doing it. The Road Transport Industry Training Board has attempted to rectify this imbalance by developing a comprehensive battery of learning packages. These deal with the knowledge aspects of many facets of managing. They have found that if these packages are given as pre-work for courses, then the courses can be devoted to considering and developing the skills for applying the knowledge. This not only shortens the courses but also makes them more effective.

Similarly, courses on coaching should concentrate on the development of the skills demanded of a good coach. One proved way of achieving this is to ask two members of a course to work on a real, unsolved problem brought by one of them. Some examples of problems which have been revealed by participants are:

1 I have appointed to my staff an ex-assistant factory commercial manager, aged 42, with 21 years service with the company.

   His job is to take over the day-to-day responsibility of the commercial training within the company and to assist the supervisory training officer in his work on courses.

   His performance so far has been established as good on the administrative side but when in the face to face training situation he totally lacks empathy and the ability to communicate on a two way basis. His physical appearance, of a severe school master, does not help either

2 We recruit customer service operatives from the best labour available. We give meticulous product training and training in the handling of potential problems. Furthermore, we give coaching in the handling of customer relationships by accompanying operators on their calls. We aim to leave them apparently fully competent to handle most situations. However, all too often their solo calls result in dissatisfied and frustrated customers. This involves further visits (at further expense) to rectify what should be well within the operator's ability to handle competently on the initial visit

3 I manage a comparatively small section of a company. Usually the only promotion line is external to the section. Staffing is tight and if a new member of staff is appointed his training imposes an added burden on the rest of the staff.

Such a vacancy has occurred and there are two applicants. My problem is which to select? 'A' has lower potential but adequate calibre and will probably find his level and stay. 'B' is a high flyer; eventually he will probably be an asset to the group, but may not stay with the section long enough after having been trained and gained experience to repay the investment in terms of the time and effort required in his training.

The 'coach' has the following brief:

1 to ensure that all the parameters of the problem have been stated fully
2 to help the problem owner to identify a number of courses of action which could be taken to solve the problem
3 to help him to identify which course of action he will adopt.

If the coach uses the skills of listening, questioning,

discussing and summarizing well he will find that he has been helpful in enabling the problem owner to clarify his thinking. If the coach tries to solve the problem himself or gives advice on what the problem owner should do he will find that he has been of little help.

While the two men are discussing the problem the other participants observe them on closed circuit television. Each person concentrates on one or two aspects of the form shown as figure 8.1. When the discussion is over each item on the form is used to highlight what happened during the discussion.

This method of skills training has proved beneficial in:

giving practice in the use of the skills
concentrating attention on when the use of a particular skill can help a discussion
indicating what happens if the skills are poorly used.
showing the close connection between the effective use of the skills and problem identification.

This leads us back to what the individual manager can do to improve his abilities as a coach. The following appears to be the sequence of actions required:

1 commit oneself to the proposition that coaching will make one's own job easier in the long run, but requires much time and conscious effort to begin
2 create the opportunities to coach
3 consider the skills required to coach well and then develop them by constant practice
4 after a coaching session review your own progress personally
5 continue the process until it becomes your natural way of managing.

Figure 8.1
Coaching Skills Exercise—Observation Guide

1	Question Type—Record Number	Open Closed Leading Summarizing
2	Record length of time of each separate speaking contribution	(record on separate sheet)
3	*Communication of problem* Did the problem owner define the real problem a) initially? b) eventually?	
4	What percentage of factual information was elicited? How did it compare to percentage of opinion?	
5	What other areas might have been usefully pursued?	
6	How did the coach help the problem owner to analyse the problem?	
7	How did the coach encourage the problem owner to reach a solution?	
8	Did the coach try to impose or suggest his own solutions? If so, what effect did this have?	
9	What course(s) of action emerged at the end of the discussion?	
10	Were there instances of obvious non-listening by either party? If so, what effect did these have?	
11	Was the discussion useful? How?	
12	How often did the coach summarize? If so, how did this help the discussion?	

For those who like mnemonics, figure 8.2. may be of value. The main skills of coaching discussed in detail in chapters 6 and 7 are summarized below:

Observation: Look critically at your own work and ask whether some of it could not be done by a subordinate.

Listening: Plan your listening by:

Listening for the main points.

Reviewing what has been said.

Thinking ahead to anticipate the speaker's next point, and look at the speaker while he is talking. His gestures and facial expressions may supplement his words.

Appraisal: Ensure that your subordinate really understands any points you make.

Discussion: Remember that you are engaged in a dialogue—not a lecture. Ask questions with a low structure in order to draw out the subordinate's views. Summarize progress at regular intervals.

Figure 8.2. Mnemonic for coaching

C — Confidence: do you display confidence in your subordinate's abilities to perform tasks—if not, why not?

O — Objectives: are they clearly defined for yourself and your subordinates?

A — Analysis: are you analysing the real needs of your subordinates and their jobs?

C — Competence: are you competent in the skills of coaching?

H — Habit: is coaching a regular habit and do you make full use of all opportunities to coach?

I — Information: do you know how your subordinates are progressing and do you pass to them all the information they should know?

N — Next: have you planned or are you planning the next objective, task, stage of development, etc?

G — Guidance: are you giving your subordinates the guidance that they need?

Delegation: Be clear about which responsibilities you are proposing to delegate. Discuss these fully with your subordinate. Ensure that he has sufficient resources to be able to succeed in accomplishing the new tasks. Ensure that he has sufficient control information to enable him to monitor progress. Train and coach him in any new knowledge or skills which he will require in order to be able to undertake his wider responsibilities.

The health of any organization depends primarily on the abilities and attitudes of those who work for it. It is, therefore, an integral part of any manager's job to play his part in fostering knowledge, skill and a sense of purpose in those who work for him. Conversely his own attitudes and expectations can be influenced for the well-being of the organization by his own subordinates. His skill as a coach will provide a major means for the achievement of these objectives.

CHAPTER 9

Coaching: a case study

What follows is an account of the way in which one of the regional managers of an industrial training board, responsible for the work of several field training advisers, coached a subordinate in the skills of report writing. This should serve as a useful illustration of coaching practice.

The regional manager's responsibilities include the development of sound relations between the board and a number of large companies in his industry, each of whom may have establishments in various parts of the country. The board visits a number of these establishments to assist the management in their survey of training needs and to assess the amount of levy abatement to which they are entitled. The regional manager has assigned one of his staff to consider the individual reports on the establishments of one company and to write a report to the parent company outlining the board's view of the organization of training within the company.

The training adviser had prepared his report and sent it to his manager for approval. The manager wished to rearrange the draft to bring out the main points with greater precision. The following discussion took place between the two men:

Manager: I've read your draft with interest but there

are a number of points which I think we should discuss.

Training adviser: (in hostile manner) What's wrong with the report.

M: Well, I think the report needs some redrafting. (*The manager is not helping to remove the hostility of his subordinate! He might have done better if he had asked "What does this report say to the client?"*)

TA: It's written in our standard way. In fact it is a summary of the individual reports you asked me to consider.

M: Who is going to read this report?

TA: The company's group training manager, I suppose.

M: Yes—I wonder if the managing director will also see it.

TA: Oh I should think so. In fact it's for that reason I've watered down some of the points we might make. After all we mustn't forget the political implications of being frank.

M: Let's be careful about this. Obviously the report has to be written in a way which will be acceptable to the company, but we must also be professionally honest. If we really believe something we must say so, and be able to support our views with facts.

TA: Yes, I agree with that. I think I may have to rewrite some parts of the report.

M: All right. But first let's look at the report as a whole. What are we trying to say to the client? (*The manager is now on the right lines. He has made his point about professional integrity, and stressed the importance of having the facts to support the views and the recommendations of the report.*)

TA: We're trying to convince them that we have a contribution to make.

M: What is the contribution?

TA: Well, that the board can help them to improve their training.

M: I wonder if that's our job.

TA: Well, isn't it?

M: No, I think it's more to help a company to think through the contribution training can make to its business performance and to suggest ways in which they can help themselves.

TA: Yes, I agree.

(The manager has taken the opportunity to clarify the role of the board. Clearly some clarification was required.)

M: Good. Well how does this report meet those objectives? (*At this point the training adviser spent five minutes outlining in detail the points made in the report. He gave no indication of those major points which would have led the company to think about its training system in the round. His manager listened, without interrupting. He wished to clear the way for his next, vital, question.*)

M: There's a great deal of detail there. Does the company have a framework within which to plan its training activities?

TA: Not really. I've been kind to them. For example, there's no overall analysis of training needs.

M: Should there be?

TA: Yes, of course.

M: All right. Isn't that one thing we should say?

TA: Yes, I think so.

M: What other points are important? (*The manager has now managed to get his TA to think in terms of strategy. His TA then mentioned a number of matters such as the need for work study and for improved methods of production which would be of value to the company.)*

TA: To what extent should we be involved in aspects of management which may not strictly be a training board function?

M: That depends on whether a training need is exposed. For example, in this company, do managers require to learn more about work study?

TA: Yes, undoubtedly. If they did the company might be able to make substantial progress.

M: Well, there's another general point we ought to make. It could form part of our comments on management development. *(The manager is drawing out ideas from his TA and summarizing the conversation at regular intervals.)*

TA: There's another general point to do with organization. The company has taken over a number of small firms and these just don't accept the need to introduce any of the group's systems.

M: Should we mention this?

TA: I think so. It would emphasize the need for management development throughout the group. They have a good system for craft training, but they don't really accept the need for supervisory or management training. *(At this stage the manager asked the TA to draw an organization chart.)*

M: Good. Now let's look at this in the round. Surely the group needs to think of a comprehensive training system, as well as the needs of each establishment?

TA: You're right. They have systematic training but it is at a low level. There is very little done at higher levels. *(The manager has led his TA to think in terms of group needs, and the TA's last comment indicates that he has grasped the point.)*

M: Are you saying that the group hasn't got the foundations on which to build a good comprehensive system of training? Is that fair comment?

TA: I think it's fair but I don't know if I want to say so. It's not an easy thing to phrase tactfully. How would one express it? (*Notice the manager has ensured that the TA still accepts responsibility for writing the report. It is to be signed by the TA and therefore he must consider the best way of expressing his ideas. But he is asking for help—a good use of superior by a subordinate.*)

M: Let's not discuss the actual wording for the moment. I'll have a few ideas when we discuss the report in detail. But we can't avoid making these general points about the relationship of training to the company's business needs.

TA: That's just what I'd hoped you were going to say. (*It wasn't, but no matter. The TA then summarized the general points. He's getting the idea.*)

M: Let me show you what my view of this report is. (*He then outlined the main sections. This was a necessary piece of help for the TA.*)

TA: I think that's right.

M: If we submit a report on these lines will we be discussing anything which you haven't mentioned in general terms to the company? There are three main topics I think we should mention. (*He stated them*). I'm still not too clear what you want to say about management and supervisory training?

TA: I've mentioned all these matters, but I didn't get an enthusiastic response. Perhaps that's why I was diffident about putting them in the report. I think we should . . . (*Here the TA summarized the main points, thus indicating his acceptance of the manager's outline. It was a long summary but it did not give the impression that the TA would be able to express what he wanted to say in a succinct piece of writing.*)

M: Can I ask you to summarize in a few words what you really want to say?

TA: I don't want the sack!

M: No, but we must say what we believe to be true. (*He then summarized for the TA because the TA made no further comment.*)

M: I think you'd better make a note of these points. Your draft report doesn't really stress the need for the company to think in terms of a comprehensive training system.

TA: I agree with you entirely. But we're going to rewrite this report. It needs to dovetail training into the needs of the organization.

M: Is that what you want to say?

TA: Yes.

M: Well then, let's look at the possible structure of the report.

TA: I'd like to see it shorter.

M: Well let's write down what we should say and let the length look after itself. (*The draft report was too short and one of the manager's aims was to expand it. However, he has wisely avoided an argument on this point. If he continues in this way the TA will find that he has to write a longer report to cover all the points.*)

M: What I should like is to get clear in my own mind what we should say. It's your report and you will have to make the alterations if there are any. All I've done is go back to first principles.

TA: I think I made a mistake, trying not to upset the client.

M: I can understand that. It's possible to make the report constructive and helpful. Remember it's a report from the board to the company, not from you to one man. (*This exchange resulted from the TA looking somewhat disconsolate at the prospect of rewriting the whole report. He didn't express this in words, but the manager interpreted correctly some of the TA's facial expressions. The good coach looks as well as listens!*)

TA: Who is going to read this report? We want the managing director to read it, so we'll have to write it with that in mind.

M: That's why the report may have to be longer rather than shorter. Let's look in more detail at the broad structure of the report and put down some subheadings to each section. (*They then did this.*)

TA: Mr X said he didn't think it necessary for us to put down our findings.

M: Well I think we ought to put down the main findings because they form the basis on which we shall make our comments and recommendations. (*The meeting by now had lasted 1½ hours, so the manager suggested a short break.*)

TA: I think this introduction I wrote to the draft report is wrong in view of what w⟨'ve been saying. We've got to word it in such a way that the MD will see that we're talking about a comprehensive training system.

M: OK. Let's rewrite it. Let's look at your original phrasing. (*At this point the manager gave the TA the help in phrasing for which he had asked earlier in the meeting.*)

TA: That's a great help. Now let's look at the findings. I think we should . . .

And so the two men continued until the framework of a new, longer, and much better report had been hammered out. Notice how the manager had guided the discussion skilfully so that towards the end the training adviser was taking the initiative. During the meeting the manager had made good use of the various skills of coaching. He had listened, asked questions, observed the reactions of his training adviser and had given information and knowledge when it was required. Most important he had avoided the trap of rewriting the report for him. At the end of the meeting the training adviser still felt that it was his report, but that it had been much improved as a result of the discussion.

CHAPTER 10

Is performance appraisal necessary?

If a chapter on performance appraisal in a book about coaching is a cause for surprise then at least your attention will have been drawn to one of the most important principles of good coaching practice. Coaching is a continuous process, not a once a year exercise. It is true that there are managers who regard a performance appraisal interview as an opportunity to coach and a chance to stand back from daily routine and look at the overall task in discussion with their colleagues. Excellent as this approach is, a once a year day must be supplemented by continuous on-the-job coaching. With the constraint of needing to complete the appraisal form by a given date, this kind of review session imposes a time limit on the coaching, and the question arises as to whether it is the best method of allowing managers and subordinates the opportunity to take a detailed examination of the overall job. The successful coach acquires, through a combination of experience and instinct, the ability to sense the need for an overall examination, and he times the review session accordingly. It will be more a coincidence than timing if his view of the optimum timing coincides with the company's laid down procedures for performance appraisal.

I once had a boss who refused steadfastly to discuss

with me what he had written on my performance appraisal form. Quite reasonably he took the view that if I didn't know his view of my work from the very frequent coaching and job review sessions we had together, then I must have failed to gain anything from these meetings. He non-plussed me by stating (quite correctly) that my main interest in what he had written was to enable me to assess the likely size of my salary increase. In answer to my affirmative grin he then proceeded to explain that although it was the company's policy to take performance appraisal reports into consideration when awarding salary increases, somehow the firm's salary policy didn't match up to their brave words. So, to avoid disappointment, he refused to discuss with his men the contents of the official appraisal form. The disappointment could, of course, have worked both ways: his, because he thought I might be given more than I was worth; mine for the opposite reason.

The point of this story is that it focuses attention on a common state of affairs, namely, confusion in people's minds as to the real purpose of performance appraisal in their organizations. Dale H Scharinger [1] raised the question of how performance appraisal could fit best into a *total* management development process. Here are some of his more pungent points:

Industry is falling into the trap of grades, report cards, indefensible methods of evaluation rather than educating human beings.

The responsibilities of each manager are:

a to understand his own development needs . . . if each individual manager realizes and puts forth effort in self-development, then he, as a subordinate, will learn to accept communication as to his development needs

b communicating development needs to his

subordinates

c ... take the responsibility of coaching his subordinates on the job.

The chief criticism of formal appraisal is that it eliminates informal day-to-day appraisal and transfers it to a sterile periodic evaluation.

Thought should be given to establishing three types of appraisal: one for development purposes, another for salary, and a third for promotion.

It may be fashionable to knock performance appraisal, but we must be careful not to eliminate any advantages it has. One of these is that, well conducted, appraisal can satisfy a need for the subordinate to know how well he is performing from his boss's viewpoint.

Douglas McGregor [2] was one of the first to question the validity of appraisal procedures. His article was reprinted as a classic in September 1972, with a foreword stating: "that the ideas are not as fresh now is testimony to the wide acceptance of McGregor's belief in encouraging individuals to develop their potentialities in the organizational setting."

Since then there have been research projects, articles, and countless ideas on how to improve performance appraisal, but still we find organizations introducing the same old forms and concepts which led to the controversy in the first place. Also, as the *Harvard Business Review* points out, there has been considerable improvement in the attitude of the more progressive companies.

Many of the problems connected with peformance appraisal stem from a lack of clarity in determining what it is intended to achieve, and then an attempt to do too many things at once. Normally these include:

letting the manager know how he is getting on in the opinion of his superior (part of John

Humble's third need of a manager)

spotting talent so that good promotion prospects
are not overlooked

forming part of the input into salary review discussions

identifying the training and development needs of
the manager

standing back and reviewing progress in the job.

Consider these aims in a little more detail. If a manager has to wait for a once-a-year interview before he
knows what his superior thinks about him, then
there is something seriously wrong with the relationship between the two men. And often there is. We all
know examples of men saying "I don't know how I'm
getting on. I suppose all right because my boss doesn't
complain" or "I only see my boss when something
goes wrong". So if the aim is to communicate the
superior's view of the man's progress, performance
appraisal is not the correct way to set about it.

Talent spotting is important in large organizations, but good people readily draw attention to
themselves in small companies. Some people are
cynical about promotion anyway. If your face fits you
get promoted. Indeed part of the skill of setting up an
organization is to blend a number of people who will
work well together as a team. Individual performance merit does not of itself qualify a person to fit
snugly into a group of people at a higher level. The
man who works well with one team may not be able to
provide the awkward, balancing view which a senior
manager wishes to provide in another team. In large
companies, however, the central personnel department does need to have records of men's performance
and an assessment of their potential. People don't
change rapidly and one would have thought that a
biennial or triennial report on an individual would be
quite sufficient for this purpose. Annual, or even six

monthly reporting may be necessary for young men at the start of their careers. The objection that an annual report is required to ensure fairness and consistency can be answered by having a triennial report which is prepared by several managers with whom the man has come into contact. If a suitable job comes up between reviews a special report can be prepared.

In most companies salary increases are determined by other considerations in addition to merit. For example:

'Do we have to pay him more to keep him?'
'What will Jones say if Smith gets a larger increase than he does?'
'We couldn't possibly give him a rise of that size.'
'He's not really worth it but we'd better give him something.'

There is no need to pretend that the results of the performance appraisal play a major part in salary determination. In practice they are irrelevant except in extreme cases of outstandingly good or poor performance, and one doesn't need a performance appraisal to spot those cases. A better approach for salaries is for each boss to make and to justify salary increase recommendations for his team.

Identifying training and development needs is one of the supposed uses of performance appraisal. In some companies the training department is supposed to go through the appraisal forms and to collate the parts dealing with training needs. Knowing how these forms are often filled in I would doubt their reliability as a guide to the training policy of a company.

How many appraisal forms containing a section on training needs are filled in like this:

what aspect of the job requires improvement?
—human relations

what improvements have you planned?—better human relations

what steps have you agreed to take to help him?—a course on human relations.

If the role of the training department is to ensure that the man's real needs are met, much more information is required than is contained on the usual appraisal form. In any case I believe that the main role of a central training department is to ensure that the organization has a sound training *system*, not to provide courses for individuals. The concept of continuous coaching, if carried out well, will ensure that individual needs are identified and satisfied.

Finally, what about looking at the job as a whole? This has great merit and should be part of the normal process of managing. Job review, as it is often called, is an integral part of Management by Objectives. But job review should take place as the situation arises, not when the company's appraisal procedures demands. Later in the chapter we shall discuss how this job review process can be made part of the day-to-day coaching activity. But first let us dispose finally of annual performance appraisal by considering some of the criticisms levelled at it.

In the middle 1960s, the American General Electric Company carried out a series of studies on their appraisal programme. Some of the findings were interesting:

criticism has a negative effect on the achievement of goals

defensiveness, resulting from critical appraisal procedures, produces inferior performance

coaching should be a day to day not a once a year activity.

In a study Ken Folkes and Maurice Gubby[3] found that the most common reasons for dissatisfaction with an interview were:

the interviewer was too vague and not frank enough
the interviewer did not seem to be interested
the interview underlined the lack of career prospects
the interview promised action which was not fulfilled later.

There are countless articles written in this vein, criticising aspects of appraisal procedures and suggesting remedies, or as the cynic might suggest, palliatives. For my part, I would remove the phrase performance appraisal from the management literature and replace it by a series of procedures designed to:

encourage managers to coach
ensure that there are periodic discussions between the man and his boss about the job (job review)
ensure that basic information on suitability for promotion is held by the central personnel departments of large companies
enable reasonable and acceptable decisions to be made on salary increases.

A major aim of any appraisal process, concerned with trying to help a subordinate, should be to enable him to qualify for a good salary increase. If bosses made that clear, if they indicated that they wanted to help and not to judge, then the hidden agendas of salary, promotion or playing god on the part of the boss would be removed. Many bosses do not consider how much their subordinates need to learn in the course of doing the same job. Every time a procedure changes, a new product is introduced, or a new machine is installed, the man has a need to learn. How often do bosses help him? Write down all the changes your subordinates have had to deal with in the past year. You may be surprised how long the list becomes. Then consider the *tasks* he could have performed better. From that starting point decide what skills/knowledge would have enabled him to do better. This is the correct order for thinking about performance. Too often we start at the other end by saying 'He doesn't delegate well' or 'his communicating is poor' or 'he doesn't cooperate'. But delegating, communicating, cooperating are only means to an end, and unless we have defined the tasks which could have been performed better we can't really help a man to recognize that he has something to learn.

The Steetley Company Ltd, has been modifying its performance appraisal system over a period of five years. Today the three elements of salary review, promotion potential and personal development have been entirely separated from each other. Indeed as figure 10.1 on pages 133–136 shows the development aspect is no longer called appraisal but rather the company's Management Development Plan'. A feature of this plan is that as item H on figure 10.1 shows career guidance has to be discussed at a separate meeting. The company has thought out its strategy so well that its own internal documentation 'a fresh look at annual appraisal' is reproduced in full as figure 10.2 on pages 137–139. Notice particularly that under the heading "What's in it for you?"'improved salary and career promotion are linked to the *results* of management development and are no part of it. Figure 10.3 on page 140 is 'A Checklist for Managers' holding a management development interview. The whole purpose is neatly summarized at the bottom in the words 'a joint exercise aimed at causing

Figure 10.1
The Steetley Company Ltd

MANAGEMENT DEVELOPMENT PLAN

Department, etc	Name	Job Title

A. Last year's training and development

1. WHAT FORMAL TRAINING COURSES WERE ATTENDED?—and what was gained?

2. WHAT OCCURRED IN THE JOB TO CHALLENGE THE EMPLOYEE?—look at changes in responsibilities, job circumstances and special events.

B. Last year's performance

3. WHAT WERE THE EMPLOYEE'S MOST SIGNIFIC-ANT ACHIEVEMENTS?—single out the most outstanding 2 or 3 items.

4. WHAT **TASKS** CAUSED THE EMPLOYEE MOST DIFFICULTY?—single out the most obvious 1 or 2 items and try to identify cause.

C. Next year's challenges

5. WHAT IS LIKELY TO HAPPEN TO CHALLENGE THE EMPLOYEE?—i.e. what changes, in responsibilities/job circumstances or special events of the type that occurred last year, are likely to happen next year?

D. Deciding next year's development priorities

Now that you have reviewed last year's challenges/difficulties and anticipated next year's changes you need to decide where to **concentrate** your development effort. Your broad options are:

a) Solve current difficulties (Q4)
b) Prepare for anticipated changes (Q5)
c) Seek to introduce new challenges in the form of new tasks or greater responsibility for existing task areas

You should focus on whichever of these three 'development steps' is likely to give the greatest mutual 'pay-off' in the particular circumstances. Once you have located the right development step you should specify this as a task(s) and/or performance standard(s) that the employee is to achieve and write it up overleaf (Q6) in the form of a job objective(s). The more specific you can get at this stage, the easier it will be to work out **how** you will cause it to happen (Stage F).

E. Next year's development objective(s)

6. WHAT IS IT NOW AGREED THAT THE EMPLOYEE WILL DO IN THE JOB?—that will require special effort to achieve.

F. Next year's development programme—to achieve the development objective

7. WHAT FORMAL TRAINING IS REQUIRED?—i.e. such as may be gained from courses/books.

8. WHAT ADDITIONAL 'JOB KNOWLEDGE'/INFORMATION IS REQUIRED?—e.g. policies, systems, procedures, methods, data, situations, etc.

9. WHAT OTHER ACTION IS REQUIRED?—by way of setting up, coaching, monitoring, etc., indicate who will be responsible for taking the action and by what date.

G. Signatures

Employee Date	Manager Date	Manager's Manager	Date

H. Career guidance

The employee has specially requested guidance in connection
with future career.
* We have arranged to discuss this on ....
* We have made an appointment for the employee to discuss
  this with ....
  on ....
  * delete as appropriate

development to happen'. This is a far cry, and a welcome step forward, from traditional appraisal
approaches.

Performance review

An effective performance review system will have as
its aims:

> to enhance the commitment/involvement of the
> subordinate in striving to achieve defined objec-
> tives.
> to help him to learn and to think more clearly
> to compare his perspective of his job with the pers-
> pective of his boss
> to enable the men to share their knowledge and
> experiences
> to establish a firm base from which the man can
> develop his abilities.

136

Figure 10.2
The Steetley Company Ltd

THE MANAGEMENT DEVELOPMENT INTERVIEW

Introduction
The Group first introduced management development, based on annual appraisal, in 1973. Since then we have been continually revising our ideas and forms in the light of experience and the opinions of line managers. These revisions have taken us further and further away from making **judgements** about people and towards **helping** them to develop in and from their present jobs.

What is management development really about?
You can be said to have developed when you are DOING something that you could not or did not DO before. Thus the key issues are:

What you ARE DOING
What you SHOULD BE DOING   IN YOUR **PRESENT** JOB
what you COULD BE DOING

Attending courses does not constitute development; this is merely a **means** of helping you to DO better in the job. Promotion is not development; it is a **consequence** of your having developed.

What do we really want out of 'appraisal'?
Using annual appraisal to fulfil several objectives frequently leads to confusion and the achievement of none. Our revised appraisal format is concerned **only** with:

- helping you to cope with existing challenges;
- introducing you to new challenges in your present job; if you are ready for them, if you want them, and if they aren't happening in the normal course of things.

If these simple objectives can be achieved we should find that we are developing a fully competent and responsive management team. We should also discover that the related issues of management succession and promotion can be left to the Internal Advertising Procedure.

In fact our revised 'appraisal' format is so different in aim and content to the traditional model that we have re-named it the 'Management Development Interview'

What's in it for you?

Most employees want to succeed in what they are DOING and at the same time to continue to receive challenge from their work. This is, precisely, the aim of the Management Development Interview.

Naturally if you DO better or DO more you expect more pay. This is the function of the Annual Salary Review (legislation permitting) and the Job Evaluation Scheme, respectively. However both of these are concerned with the **results** of development. They are totally distinct from the Management Development Interview, the purpose of which is to **cause** development to happen.

What's in it for the boss?

In return for an initial effort in helping you to cope better or expand in your job your manager will expect:

- to have to put in less effort to assist you day by day;
- to be free to operate at the most challenging extremes of his/her own job

Why have an annual interview?

Your manager will undoubtedly respond to your successes and difficulties as they occur. Added to this there will always be something new happening to challenge you in your job. So why have an annual interview? Basically it is a stocktaking exercise; an opportunity to step aside from the tumult of activity and:

- remind yourself (and your manager) of the year's main achievements;
- reflect on any difficulties experienced and see whether these are worth a concerted effort to sort out;
- add up last year's challenges, look forward to next year's and assess whether there is enough happening to keep you stimulated;
- decide whether next year's development priority should be to sort out difficulties, prepare for known changes or deliberately import a new challenge;
- agree a plan of action to achieve your priority.

In short, a review of the past leading to a plan for the future.

What should happen at the interview?

The interview is a discussion between you and your manager aimed at the joint completion of a 'Management Development Plan'.

138

To ensure that the discussion is firmly grounded on what is DONE in your job, you should have before you a list of duties/responsibilities or objectives. If this type of document does not exist a simple list should be agreed at the outset of the discussion.

The Plan has been designed to provide a logical, non-threatening discussion format. **If the questions are taken in turn you should arrive, naturally, at a meaningful action programme**.

Since the process has been designed mainly for your benefit you will be encouraged to do most of the talking.

Your manager might decide to complete the 'diagnostic' stages (A-D) and the 'action' stages (E and F) on different occasions. This could produce a more considered response.

Who sees the Plan?

The Plan is first and foremost a reference document for you and your immediate manager. Your manager's boss has the right to see the Plan to ensure that there is sufficient development taking place in the wider management unit of which you are a member. Your Personnel Manager will need to see all Plans to prepare next year's programme of formal training based on the answers to Question 7.

Steetley Head Office's only role is to consider the quality and quantity of development taking place **across the whole organization** and to ensure that the documentation and Groupwide training activity is adequate. Head Office will not normally need to see individual Plans.

A copy of the form will be retained on your personal file as a record of your development with Steetley.

*   *   *

The process described above should assist in the steady growth of your managerial capacity. Beyond this it is up to you to secure any promotion via the Internal Advertising Procedure. However, we recognize that Steetley is a complex organization and that individuals will from time to time need guidance to identify the possible direction of their next move. If this happens to be your problem you are invited to raise it with your manager at the Management Development Interview and a separate appointment will be made for you to discuss the question with your manager, or the Division or Group Personnel Department, as appropriate.

Aspects of the interview	Points to remember
Objectives	To assist in the development of employees by helping them to cope with existing challenges and introducing new challenges where appropriate.
Preparation for the interview	1. Compile a list of the employee's main duties or better still get him/her to complete a Job Development Form. This will help ensure that the interview is based on fact/performance. 2. Consider the points you might wish to raise under questions 2, 3, 4, & 5.

The interview . using the plan	1. Have the plan on the table and complete as the discussion progresses - a joint approach.
	2. Follow the questions on the plan in sequence, it has been designed as a logical process.
	3. It might be useful to break the interview after question 5 the fact finding stage, before going into questions 6 - 9 the planning stage, to allow time for reflection and consideration.
	4. The difficult questions are:-
	    Q.4 - encourage the **employee** to answer this question
	      - deal only with **incidents and fact**, avoiding generalities and personality issues **at all costs**
	      - encourage the **employee** to suggest the cause of the problem
	      - if it appears that even after some deliberation the employee does not acknowledge the problem, be prepared to move onto the next question and deal with any unresolved performance problem in the normal managerial manner, i.e. set clear performance standards and simply require that they are attained.
	    Q.6 - This statement should:-
	      - focus on what you want the employee to DO in the job
	      - be sufficiently stimulating to cause some real development to occur
	      - be as specific as possible
	    Part F - the more specific your answer to question 6 the easier it will be to deal with these questions
	    Q.7 - this is an area where help can be obtained from your Personnel Department.

. handling the discussion	1. Ask questions rather than make statements. 2. Ask open questions where possible, e.g. "What do you ....?" 3. Reflective questions assist the process, e.g. "How do you think you could have solved that problem?" 4. Summarise frequently. 5. Try to be positive. Negative interviews can lead to poor performance. If you are unable to identify any difficulties to be overcome or new challenges which can be introduced, i.e. there can be no further development, consider the use of a career guidance interview with the Divisional Personnel Manager or the Group Personnel Department, who have particular expertise in this area.

These aims can be achieved by:

1 looking forward to what changes and improvements are required. This entails some consideration of what has happened in the period preceding the review
2 indicating clearly to the subordinate what are the expectations of the boss
3 considering the resources required to achieve the performance objectives agreed between the two men
4 identifying any special learning needs of the subordinate which have not been brought out in the day-to-day coaching which has taken place.

A successful job review is essentially a forward looking exercise which only draws on past experience, and past achievements or failures as a means of clarifying future action. Success lies in the extent to which the boss can establish an atmosphere of mutual confidence and respect between himself and his subordinate. If he hasn't established this in his day-to-day dealings, he will have difficulties when he tries to achieve it at a job review. Thus job review and coaching are closely interlinked. The formal review is an opportunity for both men to take stock in the fluid situation of everyday management decision making.

The formal review meeting, held at regular and agreed intervals, is essentially a dialogue between the job holder and his superior. A basic purpose is to review the contribution of the *job* in terms of:

progress in completing agreed contributions to the improvement plans and objectives of the job holder *and* the group of job holders of which he forms a part

    modification of the objectives through improve-
      ment or adjustment of the standard of perfor-
      mance required
    dropping inappropriate or non-priority objectives
      and agreeing the next plan for improvement.

In carrying out this review its historical aspect is of least importance. The priority is forward planning. The review also provides an excellent opportunity and the correct environment for the superior to provide coaching and guidance. Thus job review has no links with Performance Appraisal which, of necessity, has overtones of criticism and defensiveness, conditions under which coaching cannot take place.

A job review meeting cannot be staged in a hurry. Adequate preparation by both the job holder and his superior is essential. There must be several days' notice of the superior's intention to hold a job review. There are also instances when the job holder initiates a job review by asking his manager to hold one. The willingness of the job holder to do this indicates the nature of the sound relationship existing between the two men. The man has felt a need and his superior has reacted to it.

Figure 10.4 shows the pattern of a typical well-conducted job review. Notice that the job holder initiates the review part of the meeting. He, more than his superior, knows how well things are really going. The development part of the meeting is a dialogue between the two men with the job holder doing most of the talking.

Some of the problems which can arise

In those companies, and one hopes that they will increase in number, where some form of written objectives and standards of performance exist there

142

Figure 10.4 *The pattern of a job review*

Phase of Meeting	Initiative by		Principal Activity	Balance of time
	Job Holder	Superior		
R E V I E W			1 Review overall progress in 3 or 6 month period. 2 Review key tasks. 3 Check control data.	$\frac{1}{4}$ to $\frac{1}{3}$ of meeting (say 30/45 minutes)
D E V E L O P M E N T			4 Identify current limiting factors.	$\frac{2}{3}$ to $\frac{3}{4}$ of meeting (say 60/90 minutes)
			5 Develop next improvement plan from balance of prior or new suggestions of action to be taken	
			6 Agree revision of standards of performance.	
			7 Identify learning needs.	
			8 Personal coaching by superior.	

may be a misdirected determination to review the documentation of the objectives word by word. The mechanistic nature of this type of review, used in many early job review meetings, is shown in the form of an algorithm in figure 10.5. Performance standards are essential to good managerial practice, but they need to be used with an understanding of their limitations.

A good performance standard should reveal, both for the manager and for his subordinate, what constitutes a good or satisfactory performance and what does not. In real life, however, reality is seldom black or white. There are degrees of satisfactory and unsatisfactory. Anyone who has worked in the field of quality control is well aware of this problem. So when reviewing the results achieved against the previously expected standards of performance, there will in practice be an element of judgement. This is no bad thing. The important point about having

143

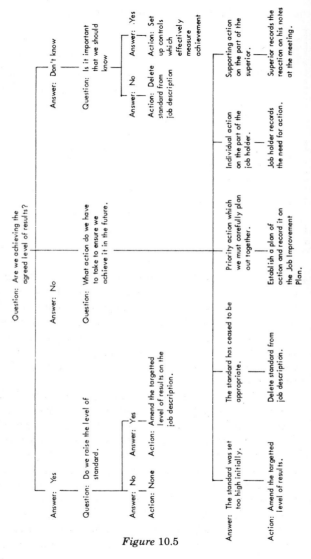

Figure 10.5

The question, answer and action structure of early job review meetings

performance standards is that they enable subjective judgements to be made with greater justification.

Similarly in reviewing performance against standard, both men need to keep in the forefront of their minds the relationship between actual performance on the job and its effect on the performance of the group or unit of which this job forms a part. There is no point in one man achieving his results if he does so at the expense of the unit as a whole. The truth of this has been recognized by Management by Objectives practitioners. A matrix form of objective setting for a whole unit is now commonly used. This means that the results required by the unit are identified along one axis of the matrix; the other axis is a list of managers who comprise the unit. When a manager's responsibility has a major (as opposed to a marginal) effect on the desired result a tick is placed in the matrix. In this way realistic standards of performance of each manager can be agreed with a view to their effect on unit performance as a whole. Figure 10.6 shows schematically how this matrix works.

The use of this kind of matrix enables both parties to discuss frankly the effect of the way in which the manager achieves his performance targets. He may have done so, but in a way which prevents others in the unit performing well. This may stem from personality problems which need to be aired and resolved.

Finally, the achievement of satisfactory performance depends on adequate resources being available to the manager. This includes more than physical resources. It implies that the man himself has the knowledge and the skills required, that these are present in his subordinate and that his superior makes his own expertise available if need be. In this way a job review can, and should, cover both the development of the human resources necessary to

Figure 10.6 *Responsibility influence matrix*

RESULT

MANAGER	PRODUCTION AMOUNT	QUALITY	COST	LABOUR RELATIONS	PURCHASING	PLANNING	etc	etc	etc
A	✓	✓		✓					
B	✓	✓	✓	✓				✓	
C			✓		✓				
D	✓					✓		✓	
E		✓	✓						
F	✓	✓	✓	✓					✓
G	✓			✓		✓	✓		

achieve targets, and the method whereby the fund of experience and expertise within the business as a whole is available for use by the job holder.

So far we have mentioned only those problems of job review which can arise from a too rigid adherence to a discussion of previously agreed performance targets. A further problem can stem from the superior manager playing too strong a role in the job review discussion. To do so may put his subordinate on the defensive. If this happens we are merely reproducing, under another name, the attitudes and perceptions of performance appraisal. A manager can avoid these hazards if he encourages the job holder to take the initiative along the lines outlined in figure 10.4. This does not imply that the superior manager should lose control of the situation and blindly follow wherever his subordinate leads. His role as superior is to judge the progress being made and through his skills as a coach to ensure that all critical items are discussed within a realistic time scale.

The amount of time required for a job review will vary with the frequency with which they take place, the previous understanding and relationship between the two men, and the measure of change in the job situation. Figure 10.4 suggests that a time of about two hours is appropriate in most situations, but there will be occasions when considerably longer is required because one or more items demand detailed examination. It is important to remember that one of the major purposes of the review meeting is to stand back and to look at the job as a whole. If too much time is spent on one item there is a danger that this purpose will be defeated, or insufficient attention will be paid to other equally important aspects of the job. It is therefore a sound strategy for the boss skilfully to guide the discussion so that all the major issues have been explored within three hours. Any issues or problems which need more detailed examination should be identified and then dealt with at a separate meeting

Experience of holding job reviews has shown that there are four fundamental criteria by which success can be measured:

1 The superior and the job holder must be at ease. They must both feel free to participate and to take the initiative when they so wish. They are talking about the job and their prime interest is to take decisions which will lead to improvement. A hidden agenda which concerns some kind of appraisal of the job holder's strengths and weaknesses should be suppressed ruthlessly unless the job holder himself raises these matters in relation to the needs of the work situation. So a job holder may, by skilful guidance, be led to say, "I must try

harder to cooperate with X". It is inappropriate for a superior to say, "Most of the trouble stems from your inability to cooperate with others". Even if this is true it is a matter to be dealt with at a later coaching session. Brought up at a job review it will serve only to sour the atmosphere, unless the two men know each other very well, and there is a great deal of mutual respect.

2 The review must be arranged for a clearly defined purpose. If this is made clear both men will prepare carefully for it.

3 The discussion should be directed to the future, rather than become an inquisition or *post mortem*.

4 The meeting must be regarded as an integral part of the normal process of line management. It should not be something which takes place because the personnel department has laid down a procedure and a timetable.

Preparing for a job review

Prior to the review the manager/coach should have agreed a time and place acceptable to the subordinate. That arranged the subordinate should be allowed sufficient time and opportunity to review the work done since the last review, to raise current work problems and to suggest what help is required and how it may be provided.

Alcan-Booth Ltd have introduced a self-appraisal review form (figure 10.7) which is designed to help the subordinate to clarify his thinking in preparation for his job performance discussion with his boss. It is instructive to quote from the company's staff development guide on the subject of appraisal and review:

148

Principles

In order that objectives of the staff development scheme should be met the following principles must be understood and observed when conducting appraisals of subordinates:

1 That appraisals are part of a continuous process.
2 That appraisals should concentrate on performance, improvement, strengths and commitments and not upon personality unless results are being impeded.
3 That self-appraisal should be encouraged and form an essential prelude and basis for discussion.
4 That attack countered by defence is not a successful appraisal interview technique.
5 That frequency of formal review will vary with the needs of the individual and extent of job change.
6 That the interests of the appraiser and appraised are best served if the record is designed for a mutual and frank discussion and not for the benefit of third parties (eg superior management or personnel records).

The back of the form (figure 10.7) invites the boss to comment on the results of the interview and to state the commitments agreed as a result of the interview.

The company has found that this procedure has improved the acceptance and relevance of 'appraisal' and that it has been welcomed by both bosses and subordinates.

The coach himself should prepare:

records of performance in the area covered by the subordinate's command

an assessment of future work load and work problems, defining possible development opportunities which the subordinate should grasp

Figure 10.7 Alcan-Booth self appraisal review

	NAME:	
	JOB TITLE:	
SELF-APPRAISAL REVIEW	DEPT.	DIVISION
	LOCATION:	DATE:
	REVIEW PERIOD:	

This form is issued to you for completion to help promote and guide a discussion between you and your manager about your job performance during the past . . . . . months. The purpose of this discussion will help you establish guide lines to improve your performance and agree steps for your development and training. The discussion should result in a clearer understanding of:

(a) The main purpose of your job, its scope and the main activities required for its accomplishment.
(b) The critical targets and tasks which are agreed by you both as necessary and achievable.
(c) The means by which you can determine your success in carrying out the agreed plans and the signalling of any obstacles.

1. Do you have a complete understanding of the requirements of your job? . . . .
   If "No", specify the areas which are not clear.

. . . .

. . . .

2. What have you accomplished during the period under review?

....

3. Mention any changes which you think could help you accomplish more in the forthcoming period.

....

4. What parts of your job do you do best? .... What parts of your job do you do worst?

....

5. Have you any skills, aptitudes or knowledge not fully used in your job? ....
If "Yes", what are they?

....

6. What training would help improve your performance in your job?

....

Signed: ....

a suitable place for the interview and make arrangements that there will be no interruptions. This latter point should be taken literally. Few things can wreck a Job Review more than a chance interruption cutting across a detailed discussion whose purpose is to achieve a consensus of opinion.

This preparation is designed to assemble facts and to structure the discussion. It is not intended to be an exercise in pre-judgement whether it be of the subordinate or of his work. The thoughts and opinions of the manager on these matters should result from the meeting.

The first job review

Job reviews, in the sense we have used the term, are not a common feature of management in most companies. A manager who is using for the first time the approach suggested here may well find that his subordinates view the session as another variation of performance appraisal. This is understandable, particularly when a job review meeting has not been preceded by the period of continuous on-the-job coaching which would make the job review appear to both men to be a natural development.

Here, then, are some points which a manager may find helpful during a first job review with a subordinate whose expectations about its purpose may be different from those of his manager:

1 The subordinate is bound to have views and opinions which differ from those of his manager, even though the problem is the same for both men. It is important that the manager understands the views of his man and refrains from appearing dogmatic.

2 The manager should demonstrate his readiness to change his opinion during the course of the discussion. This should be explicit so that his man can recognize the flexibility of his boss's thinking.

3 The manager should always be constructive. It is of little use to appear to criticize without putting forward an alternative solution for discussion.

4 Problems which arise concerning the subordinate's job should be solved if possible by the subordinate. The manager should not act as an answering machine. Frequently, the need is to determine the exact nature of the subordinate's problems as a preliminary step to solving them.

5 Examine successes as well as failures. They can more easily serve as a basis for advance.

Lack of skill on the part of the manager or the personality characteristics of the subordinate may cause the latter to react in many different ways during the review session. The following are some of the confusions that can arise:

1 The two men cannot agree about the facts. In this situation total agreement will be impossible. When the area of disagreement has been identified and agreed then the manager should be prepared to say, "We'll leave that aside and I'll check on my facts if you will check on yours."

2 The subordinate agrees with his boss too readily. In this situation it is often helpful to ask the man to summarize the discussion so far. In his summary he may indicate any reservations he has about his boss's position.

3 The subordinate passes the buck. This is a common pastime and may be justified in some circumstances. But buck passing is sterile unless it is accompanied by some plan to help the man who has the real responsibility. Therefore, the real

circumstances should be analysed and a plan of action agreed. What is the use of agreeing that the supply department is not doing a good job, unless the user is willing to help in some way to alleviate their problems. Buck passing so often implies that the other man is incompetent or not trying. This is unlikely. You aren't perfect so why assume others should be? But you can often help them to solve a problem.

4 Subordinates sometimes react emotionally. The best plan is to listen—not to argue or to disapprove. Let the emotions subside naturally. A useful adage in these circumstances is *Do not pour cold logic on hot emotions*.

5 If the subordinate is passive and unresponsive, concentrate on any matters which you know are of interest to him, even if to start with they are only of marginal importance to the job review.

Job review implies that a manager should manage essentially through self-control. The coach is there to help the man to clarify his ideas, to plan his actions and to ensure that what the man does fits into the overall requirements of the unit.

But managers are human. The more self-confident a man is, the more successful he has been in the past, the less he is likely to seek guidance without prompting unless the right environment has been established. A unit manager remains accountable for the achievements of his subordinate team even though he has delegated specific objectives and authority to them. He must be able to offer guidance, even when not requested, before a situation gets seriously off target. If this guidance is to be acceptable it should become part of day to day management through the medium of coaching. Periodical job reviews require a follow up in the daily act of managing.

1 SCHARINGER, DALE H, Performance Appraisal—A Means or an End, *Training and Development Journal,* April 1969
2 McGREGOR D, An Uneasy Look at Performance Appraisal, *Harvard Businss Review,* May 1957
3 FOLKES K and GUBBY M, Job Appraisal Reviews—Do They work?, *Civil Service Opinion,* September 1971

CHAPTER 11

Coaching and job review: a case study

In this chapter we study a case of job review in some detail in order to draw out the points made in the last chapter and to show how they can be applied in practice. Particular attention should be paid to the way in which the review is used as a coaching session. This case is based on a real situation, so the boss's statements are not all ideal.

The job under review is that of an area sales manager who reports to a regional sales manager. The results guide for the job is shown in Figure 11.1. What follows is the content of, and comment on, the job review carried out by the two men.

Boss: We agreed last week that it would be useful to have one of our regular, more structured meetings to discuss how the job is going. I've refreshed my memory by looking at the results guide we prepared together for your job, but I don't want our discussion to be backward looking. We ought to discuss what needs doing in the next six months. I say this because I know you have worked hard and I assume you know better than I do the details of what you might have done better. What I want from this meeting is the feeling that we are agreed what should be done next. (*Notice that the boss has recognized overtly that the subordinate knows more about the details of the job than he does. This is bound to be the case. A common cause of complaint by subordinates is that their superiors make comments or criticisms without understanding the full details, or on the basis of inadequate information. The boss has praised the man at the start. People do like to be told that they are trying, particularly if the praise is worked in as a part of the conversation. Right at the beginning the boss is trying to look towards the future.)*

Figure 11.1
Results guide for area sales manager

PERFORMANCE STANDARDS (ie the specific level of results we aim to maintain in each relevant key area)	CONTROLS (ie method of monitoring results)
1 *PROFIT CONTRIBUTION OF SALES* (a) Sales volume of each product code not less then 75% of budget	Monthly sales statistics
(b) Total sales volume of all products not less than 110% of budget	Monthly sales statistics
(c) Seasonally adjusted rate of growth of sales not less than 10% per year	Monthly moving annual total
(d) Proportion of sales at given levels of gross margin not less favourable than 8% of sales at gross margin above 40% 10% of sales at gross margin between 35-40% 30% of sales at gross margin between 30-35% 25% of sales at gross margin between 25-35% 15% of sales at gross margin between 20-25% 12% of sales at gross margin below 20%	(Special investigation)

PERFORMANCE STANDARDS (ie the specific level of results we aim to maintain in each relevant key area)	CONTROLS (ie method of monitoring results)
2 *SALES FORCE EFFECTIVENESS* Call Frequencies not less favourable than: 'A' class outlets 2 per month 'B' class outlets 1 per month 'C' class outlets 1 per 2 months	Sales rep statistics
(b) Sales turnover per call for each outlet to be within the range £75-£300	Sales rep statistics
(c) Average calls per month per rep is between 60-80	Analysis of black book
(d) Growth of new accounts maintained at not less than 3½% per year	Sales accounts data book
(e) Range of product codes stocked to be not less favourable than: 'A' class outlets—90% of their stock 8 or more codes 'B' class outlets—90% of their stock 5 or more codes 'C' class outlets—90% of their stock 3 or more codes	Customer record cards
3 *TRAINING AND MOTIVATION OF REPS* (a) Turnover of reps. not greater than 20% per year	Personnel return
(b) At least one rep. is capable of taking over duties of Area Manager at short notice	Judgement
(c) New reps. achieve their order value points target within 6 months	Reps check sheets
(d) Reps. are being accompanied on at least 10 of their routine calls per year as a check on their approach to the customer	Training records

PERFORMANCE STANDARDS (ie the specific level of results we aim to maintain in each relevant key area)	CONTROLS (ie method of monitoring results)
(e) Every rep. has a training and improvement plan and his performance is being reviewed at least 3 times per year	MbO record file
4 *MERCHANDISING EFFECTIVENESS* (a) Merchandising team visit outlets at not less than following frequency: 'A' class outlets 4 times per year 'B' class outlets 2 times per year	Customer record cards
(b) Outlets are displayed up to date point-of-sale aids as follows: Show Cards .... 75% Dispensers 50%	Sample observations by regional manager
5 *INTRODUCTION OF NEW PRODUCTS* (a) No new product is launched without at least 1 month's backing stock	
(b) Every rep is thoroughly acquainted with selling features of new products	
6 *MARKET INTELLIGENCE* (a) There are no sudden changes in market share/sales volume due to undetected changes in market conditions or competitors' activities	Judgement by regional manager
7 *ACCURACY OF SALES FORECASTING* (a) Actual Sales (overall) within 5% of forecast	Monthly sales statistics
(b) 75% of product codes sales within 25% of forecast	Monthly sales statistics
8 *COST OF SELLING* (a) Regional Office admin costs not more than ½% of sales	Expense budget
(b) Cost of selling not more than—% of sales	Monthly cost statement

Subordinate: That's fine by me, but I want to start with the past in order to build a base for the future. I've looked at the guide and there are still some controls which are not very reliable, and I still feel that some of the most important parts of my job are completely unmeasurable. (*If the opening remarks of the boss represent a new attitude or approach many subordinates will take time to adjust and will try to stay on familiar ground. In McGregor's terms you can't change overnight from appearing to believe in Theory X to a behaviour based on Theory Y and achieve immediate credibility with your subordinates.*)

B: You know that I have always accepted that. In fact my job is worse than yours in that respect. But by isolating what can be measured from what has to be judged, we have been able to substitute fact for opinion in quite a number of instances.

S: Yes, but I still feel that my performance is being appraised on very subjective grounds.

B: Let's forget the word appraisal. I do appraise you once a year and, admittedly, that is pretty subjective. But today we are doing what we always do when we meet and that is to discuss how the job is going. The only difference is that today we have a *check list* rather than just talking about the current crises. We don't want any interruptions for the next two hours. By the end of that time we should have made a number of decisions about what I have to do, and what you have to do, to improve results.

S: Well, I shall begin then and follow our usual routine of reading out the standard and saying whether I think it has been achieved or not.

B: I don't mind if you find that easier. But what I really want to hear is what you think ought to be done if a standard has not been achieved, or has been achieved too easily. However, play it your way if you find it easier. (*The boss has not attempted to impose his new approach on the subordinate. He is gently leading him to think forward in time.*)

S: The first one 1(a) *Sales volume of each product code not less than 75 per cent of budget*. As it is worded, we have not achieved it. There were six product codes where production let us down and we got less than 50 per cent of the budget. There were four product codes which are just not selling. The other 35 products are within our standard.

B: Let me ask two questions. Is the standard we set a good one? Do we need to take any action in view of the fact that we have not achieved the standard?

S: In answer to the first question, I think the standard is right even though I don't think we will ever achieve it. This may sound paradoxical but profit contribution is our life-blood, and I think we should set our standards high so that it will make us talk about it. In answer to the second question, I have already given this some thought and I have put up a suggestion on my action plan.

B: Good. I don't know if I really agree with you about setting unattainable standards, but that needn't hold us up now. About the action plan? Do you want to tell me what you propose to do? Is there any help I can give? (*The boss is setting up a potential coaching situation by saying, "Is there any help I can give?" He has also cast doubts on the validity of unattainable standards. He can return to this later if the opportunity occurs. At this stage a prolonged theoretical discussion on the value of unattainable standards would be inappropriate if the job review is to get under way.*)

S: Yes. I am going to remove all the sub-standard products from the shops. That will cost us £5,000.

And then I'm going to open samples to convince the store managers that we have overcome the problem. But the most important thing is for you to see the production manager and ensure that we get the right volume of product at the standard quality. Will you do this?

B: I like your ideas for immediate action. I wonder how your salesmen will react if your customers indicate that they do not wish to buy any more of this particular product because of the trouble we have been having.

S: Yes. (*Pause*) I think that's a good point which I'll have to consider. I suppose I'll have to warn them that this might happen and suggest the importance of being prepared to re-sell the product all over again, stressing all its good points.

B: Glad you thought of that. There is one other point I used to find useful in this sort of situation. One can often quote the man down the road who said "It's worth giving the product another chance."

S: Thanks for the idea; I'll pass it on. (*The boss's phrase 'I wonder how your salesmen will react if . . .' is unusual. Most bosses don't ponder, they 'tell' their subordinates. The tentative approach forces the subordinate to think and to object if he has doubts. Another useful phrase in this sort of situation is 'I wonder what would happen if . . .' In this case the subordinate has worked out the implications for himself, been given credit for his thinking and received a gratuitous (but helpful) hint from his boss. The conversation is loosening up.*)

B: OK. Let's give that a try and see how it works. Now about production. They have problems because they had a delivery of sub-standard material and it slipped through the acceptance people. Something is being done about that. They're also taking action on the volume question, but that is going to take some months to work through the system. I think you'd better assume that you're only going to get 90 per cent of what you want for the time being. Now, what does that mean for you?

S: That's trouble. I suppose I had better go round all the retailers and tell them.

B: Do we have to do that? Is there no other way round?

S: I can't think of one.

B: What would happen if we stopped trying to get new orders from retailers who don't carry these products, say for six months?

S: I wouldn't achieve my standard of performance and you'd be on to me.

B: Different circumstances would call for different standards. No, think it through seriously. (*Notice how the boss stops any time being wasted on a pointless discussion about the failings of the acceptance people. He also indicates that nothing immediate can be expected to ameliorate the poor volume of output of the product, a request made earlier by the subordinate. He pre-empts a discussion of the crying over spilt milk type and moves smartly on to getting the subordinate to think out a solution to his problem of getting only 90 per cent of the supplies he requires. For lack of any constructive ideas in response to the boss's suggestion of 'stopping trying to get new orders from retailers who don't carry the line' the subordinate takes refuge in what, we hope, is a facetious comment. The boss doesn't miss a trick. He immediately points out that performance standards aren't inviolate. Having made the point he returns rapidly to the immediate problem in hand: "No, think it through seriously."*)

S: Well (*Pause*) . . . I think that with luck there might be just enough to go round existing outlets.

Are you saying we should risk it and not tell retailers we may not meet their demands?

B: Well, I think it's worth trying. But for heaven's sake keep a close eye on it and let me know at once if you get any unforeseen problems arising. The managing director won't like it, but that is my affair not yours. Meanwhile I will keep on chasing production. (*All this is new ground for the subordinate. He still hasn't a constructive idea of his own. He accepts the boss's suggestion with misgivings: "Are you saying" etc. The boss issues what amounts to a direct instruction "I think it's worth trying" and assumes responsibility for failure provided that the subordinate immediately informs him if anything is going wrong. He can trust his man to spot serious problems. The boss knows that the MD won't like what's being done and makes it clear that he is taking full responsibility. In a coaching situation it is essential that when a direct instruction is given the subordinate is well aware of who is going to be held accountable. They will need reassurance on the role you are assuming. Perhaps the boss suddenly saw what he'd let himself in for . . . "Meanwhile I'll go on chasing production".*)

S: Right, let's look at standard 1(b) *Total sales volume of all products not less than 110 per cent of budget.* In view of what you've just said I'd better go away and re-write this. I'll try and maintain the same standard but if we're going easy on some products, I want to re-assess the potential for the others. Can I come and see you again when I've done my homework?

B: Fine. You may like to consider whether your salesmen are up-to-date on all the pre-sales information on the products you select for pushing. You yourself might have a look to see whether you have up-to-date information for all the right outlets for these products. Let's leave any other points on profit contribution of sales until you've had a re-think about the new situation. (*The subordinate wants time to think. The boss seizes the opportunity to slant his thinking: "You may like to consider . . ." and also moves the discussion on, so that every detailed item on the results guide is not discussed. He wants to ensure that every aspect of the job is covered during this meeting. Any points of detail can be dealt with later.*)

S: That's a help. Now standard 2(a) *Call frequencies not less favourable than: 'A' class outlets—2 per month; 'C' class outlets—1 per two months.* I'm afraid that we've not done very well here. We've had two representatives ill and one has left us, and we've not been able to replace them. We have two new boys who are understandably a bit slow. I should like to couple this discussion with standards 3(a) and 3(c), about staff turnover and induction training, which is not good. I think salaries might have a lot to do with it.

B: Wait, wait. Let's stick to one problem at a time, otherwise we'll fall into our old habit of arguing around a problem rather than looking at its root causes. What frequencies have we achieved over the last three months?

S: Class A: 1.3 calls per month average. Class B: 1.1 calls per month average. Class C: 0.45 calls per month average.

B: It's the important outlets we've fallen down on. I've been working out recently that over 70 per cent of our business comes from our 'A' customers, but only 10 per cent of the calls we make are to them. We need to have another look at how reps allocate their time. The marketing director has agreed that we should make an investigation and

I'm setting up a small team to do this. Part of your action plan will be to take part in this team and I'm having a meeting next week to work out details. (*The discussion is running smoothly. The boss ensures that only one point is dealt with at a time. After the stress of the discussion about the effects of the poor volume of production, he gives his man a rest by supplying his own piece of information, and his decision on action relating to call frequencies. But he hasn't forgotten the other points raised by the subordinate.*)

B: Now, let's go back to the points you raised about staff turnover and induction training. I think you put most of this down to salaries. Our salaries are not the highest I know. But also they are not the lowest. Are you sure that salaries are the only reason? (*The boss has supplied enough answers! He's back to making his subordinate think for himself.*)

S: No, I suppose not. But the training people are doing a good job.

B: Yes I think they do. One of the points the training manager was stressing to me the other day was the importance of adequate follow-up in the field.

S: It's all very well for him to say that, but I haven't the time to give extra attention to my new salesmen. Everyone gets their fair share of my time. I think it's the training department's job to bring new men up to an adequate standard before they're sent out in the field.

B: Think back. Have you ever known a training course which can equip anyone fully for a job? Isn't experience important?

S: Yes, of course it is, but I can't do much about that. It comes with time.

B: And a helping hand from one's colleagues?

S: That's true. One of the men who left remarked

that he didn't feel that he'd fitted into the team very well. I tried to reassure him by telling him that as he gained experience of our ways he'd find life easier. I suppose really I ought to spend more time with the new boys.

B: Yes I think you should. In the long run you'll make your own life easier if you do. Think about it and then come and see me again. I'd like to discuss this whole subject with you in greater depth.

S: OK. I'll do that when I've re-examined my ideas. (*So the boss has made his point by allowing the conversation to roll along and by prompting his man to think of new angles to his old problem. He's refrained from giving a lecture on the man's responsibility for the development of his subordinates. That can come later at the next meeting on the subject if it's required. It probably won't be—this subordinate is quite capable of thinking things out for himself once he's pointed in the right direction.*)

S: Now we come to *Merchandising effectiveness*. This is where I feel that we don't have good measures. We have achieved both standards 4(a) and 4(b) (with some to spare) but judged by a subjective criterion, I don't think that we are as good as our competitors. We don't seem to be getting either the shelf space or the position in the stores that we should like and the frequency of our merchandising efforts doesn't reflect the importance of the Class 'A' outlets.

B: I entirely agree. We haven't found a satisfactory way of measuring our merchandising effectiveness. This could explain why we're dissatisfied with our merchandising. But you know that as a division, we have an objective to get back the market share we've lost over the past three years. *Back to 30 per cent by the end of the year.* The means we have planned to achieve this are, first, to improve merchandising and secondly, to revamp the outdated product lines. Your next action plan can include your going on the new merchandising course and re-writing this section of your results guide. Do you believe that this is the real priority?

S: Yes I do. In fact it was my suggestion a year ago that this should happen.

B: Just refresh my memory and tell me what you would hope to get out of attending the merchandising course?

S: Well I suppose I'll get a whole lot of new ideas on how to merchandise.

B: I've looked at this new course and it's good. Specifically I think you will find the bits on making better use of shelf space and getting display space at the expense of our competitors of most value. Do you agree?

S: Yes, I do (*Note the answer to the highly structured question!*)

B: Well, when you come back from the course, come and see me with half a page of written notes on your ideas as to how we can implement what you've learned.

S: I'd like that. (*The boss is really moving things along now. Perhaps he doesn't know too much about merchandising himself. He talks a lot, but offers no guides or solutions other than sending his subordinate on a course. Suddenly the questions have become highly structured and he receives uninformative affirmative answers plus a crack about suggesting something a year ago. However, the boss does know what to do when he sends a man on a course. His question about what the subordinate hopes to get out of the course is a good one. Not surprisingly if both men are weak on*

merchandising he gets a weak answer. He does his
best to stimulate the man's interest by showing that
he's had a look at the course content, mentions two
parts of the syllabus that he hopes will be particu-
larly useful, and, most important of all, makes it
obvious that he relies on the man to brief him fully
on his return. He also wants a draft plan for
action.)

S: Turning to the 'Introduction of New Products' my
first standard 5(a) reads *No new product is*
launched without at least one month's backing
stock. We have not achieved this standard and I
can't see it being achieved in the near future.

B: What can we do to improve the situation?

S: I don't think there's much more that I can do.
I've chased the production people to the point at
which I'm considered to be a nuisance and that
is about the extent of my influence. In fact, I don't
believe I have any control over this situation
at all.

B: Is that true? Can't you delay the launch until you
have sufficient stocks?

S: No, I'm afraid not. I can't stop the ball rolling once
the marketing department has set it in motion.
Once the trade has been informed and all the
advertising and promotional activities are under
way, I have to work to the specified launch date.
In my opinion the cause of the trouble is the lack
of co-ordination between marketing and production. The factory does not get enough time and the
forecasts of quantity are often very inaccurate.

B: You're probably right and all that I can do is to
take this up with the general sales manager, but
we'll not get any immediate relief this way. Is
there nothing we can do?

S: Well, I suppose that I should ensure that none of
the salesmen are either taking orders which we

cannot meet, or giving unrealistic delivery promises for new products.

B: Yes, that is worth ensuring until we can improve the stock position. Shall we modify the performance standard to 'Order taking and delivery promise tactics based upon the stock situation are agreed with the salesmen before each new product launch?'

S: Right, and you'll see what can be done to improve the pre-launch stocks. Shall I go on to 5(b)? *Every rep is thoroughly acquainted with the selling features of new products.* I should say that, by and large, we are achieving this standard.

B: Wait a minute. What do you mean 'by and large'? I was with one of your men last month when he was trying to introduce the latest product line and he did not seem to be very knowledgeable. Based on that observation I would say that we're not achieving the standard.

S: I'm just trying to be practical here. When we hold our briefing for the reps we rarely manage to get them all together. Inevitably someone is unable to attend for one reason or another.

B: Then we should recognize what really happens and set our standards accordingly. Should we aim to get 70 per cent of reps acquainted etc . . . ?

S: No I think that I should aim to get every rep briefed and it's up to me to find a way of doing this more successfully. (*There are clearly problems connected with the launching of new products. The subordinate is moaning about it, but two deft questions by the boss bring him back to thinking about a solution which the boss accepts. The subordinate can't resist the natural human temptation to underline what the boss is going to do to help. I hope the latter made note of this! Regarding the briefing of the salesmen note how the boss, by offer-*

ing an obviously unsatisfactory solution, stimulated his man to commit himself to action.)

B: Very well, but what do we want them to know and what do we mean by thoroughly? (*The boss isn't leaving it at that. He wants to be sure that product briefing is done well.*)

S: I attend a briefing given by the brand manager and then I decide the content of the briefing to be given to the salesmen. Unfortunately the brand manager is usually too busy to come along to the sessions in which I brief the salesmen. I tell them everything that I know about the product.

B: It's important that we get this right. Perhaps next time we can agree the content of the new product briefing before you hold your meeting. By the way, is there a time consideration here? When do you brief them and when should you do it?

S: We don't get the necessary selling aids and product documentation until a week before the launch and so we can't afford to do the briefing much before that, and I'm not sure that it would be desirable. Perhaps two weeks before would be better.

B: OK. Let's sum up by saying that the standard should read 'Every rep receives instruction in the new product features according to an agreed brief at least two weeks before the launch.'

S: Yes, that's better. (*The boss had got what he wanted. He has made it obvious that he wants to discuss the product briefing with the man before the reps are informed. He wasn't heavy handed, and by asking relatively lowly structured questions picked up the man's obvious desire that someone (the brand manager) should help him with his briefing. The boss offered his help instead.*)

S: Shall I go on now? Standard 6(a) *There are no*

sudden changes in market share/sales volume due to undetected changes in market conditions or competitor's activities.

B: Well, did we achieve it or didn't we?

S: This standard is a matter for your judgement, it's not really for me to say whether or not it has been achieved. Do you think we have achieved it?

B: This is a difficult one. I cannot think of any changes which have occurred during the last three months, but I'm not confident that we're getting the market intelligence we need.

S: It's a very broad field and I must say I'm not too clear as to what is required. If I am to brief the salesman you'll have to be more specific about the information you're interested in.

B: You've thrown the ball in my court so you'll have to give me time to think about this one. I'll draft a check list of the important items of market and competitor activity in which we're interested and for which we need an early warning system. Then we'll discuss it. Let's leave No 7 (accuracy of sales forecasting) and go on to 8(a) *Regional Office Administration costs not more than ½ per cent of sales. (The relationship between the two men is sound. The subordinate has no hesitation in putting the boss on the rack and the latter accepts the position. He's given himself some work to do for another meeting. Presumably item 7 is connected with item 6 and can be left till later. This is a good example of how a coach can learn from his subordinates.)*

S: I think we were mistaken in putting this in. I never get the figures and even if I did, I can't control them.

B: It's not like you to be so dogmatic. Have you had a row recently with the head of sales administration section?

S: Well, yes. I got on to him and said it was time I got the analysis I wanted on time. He actually had the cheek to ask me if I really needed them.

B: Come on, calm down. Remind me what analyses you asked for.

S: Well, I asked for the analyses of sales by product type and outlet; number of calls and the order/call ratio; cost per call; information on competitors' activities and the range of their new products; changes in market condition, such as decrease in the number in my area.

B: Are all these analyses really worthwhile? I mean do you take action as a result of having them all?

S: Well no. The sales by product type, the order/call ratio and cost per call are vital but I like to get the other information because it gives me useful background information.

B: I can see why you need the background information but couldn't you get it another and cheaper way.

S: I can't think of one.

B: Well, Bill and John had the same problem and they are trying to get the information from other sources. For instance they are getting their salesmen to give them information on competitors' activities, and I understand there is other information they are managing to glean from the trade press. Why don't you go and see them and find out how it works. You never know you might get an idea which will help to reduce the costs even more. This really is important because we've got to reduce administration costs and one important contribution to doing this is for all area managers to reduce their demands. Don't get me wrong. I know you need information. All I want you to think about is ways of getting it more cheaply.

S: Fair enough, that does put it in another light. I'll go to see Bill and John. I suppose I'd better go and see the head of administration as well.

B: I'd like that. I didn't suggest it because I didn't want you to go and have a row.

S: Point taken, I'll treat him gently. (*There's a lot going on here. Notice how the boss calms the man down by asking him a question demanding a factual answer "Remind me what analyses you asked for." Then he makes a slip, "Are all these analyses really worthwhile?", but recovers by asking if they lead to action. If he hadn't added the last few words he'd probably have been treated to another emotional outburst! The boss accepts the need for the background information and sends the man off to Bill and John to learn how they solved the problem. In this mood his subordinate is likely to learn more from his peers than he will from his boss. At the end of this interchange the man has calmed down sufficiently to offer to go and have another talk with the head of administration. This highlights another important point. Many so called inter-personal problems arise from work problems. Find a means of solving the latter and the former often take care of themselves. In this case the boss has focused attention clearly on the work need: "All I want you to think about is ways of getting it more cheaply.")*

B: Now have you any other problems we haven't discussed?

Perhaps there were, but we'll leave this job review here. No doubt at the end of the meeting one or other of the men summarized the action on which they had agreed.

CHAPTER 12

Using coaching skills in the employment interview

By now the reader will have recognized that the skills we have discussed in this book have a wider application than solely in the context of management coaching. Indeed they are skills which are used in everyday life by all of us. The question is not 'should we learn the skills?', but rather how well and how appropriately do we use them?

This chapter considers the use of the skills in the context of the Job Selection interview where the interviewer is attempting to glean information from a candidate. Successful job interviews are a discussion between two people about the suitability of one of them for a vacancy. The interviewer tries to allow the candidate to present himself, and his qualifications and experience, in an accurate fashion in relation to the position for which he has applied. In this way the interviewer can assess the likelihood of the candidate being more or less suitable than other applicants. The type of vacancy we will consider is for an executive position, but much of what is written applies in principle, if not in detail, to job interviews at lower levels.

We are considering the initial interview, ie a short list of say 5–10 people from perhaps 20–100 applicants. The interview time available may be only about one hour. It is essential, therefore, that the time available is spent in the most profitable manner. Most job interviews fail at this first hurdle for they are constructed to enable the interviewer to assess the suitability of candidates, without giving the candidate a realistic opportunity to indicate exactly how he can match the job requirements. In my view a major reason why successful candidates so often fail to live up to the expectations they have aroused at interviews is that the job interviewer does not engage in a true discussion with them. Instead they attempt to match what the candidate says against their own judgement of what the job requires. What they should be doing is discussing the job with the candidate in a way which allows him to indicate how his experience will equip him for his new tasks if he is appointed.

To achieve this aim pre-supposes that the applicant possesses some detailed knowledge about what the job entails. Although it is reasonable to expect a candidate to discover for himself general facts about the organization, for example its financial performance, there is no way the ordinary external applicant can discover exactly what the vacant post entails. Normally he is given very little information on this aspect before the interview, so that much of the limited interview time may be spent by the candidate trying to work out how he can present the relevant data about himself in a way which will assist the interviewer to make a judgement.

We are in a similar dilemma to that facing appraisers where there is the element of playing god and trying to get a good salary increase. The way out which we proposed in the appraisal situation was to channel discussion into consideration of work tasks and the skills and knowledge demanded to perform well. It would be idle to strive for this outcome in an interview situation because the interviewer is of necessity playing god, and the interviewee is assessing whether he wants the job and, if he does, is attempting to present himself in a favourable light. Despite these drawbacks there is no excuse for interviewers hiding facts about the job from applicants, or giving those facts in sufficient time to allow the candidate to prepare himself.

In summary, the interview should be a discussion about a candidate's suitability for a vacancy, based on shared knowledge about the demands of that vacancy. Because time is limited applicants should come to the interview in possession of as many relevant facts as possible. When this happens the available time can be spent discussing the candidate's qualifications, skills and experience in relation to those facts. This implies that the interviewer should have undertaken considerable homework about the tasks to be performed. In my view the results of this homework should be sent to short listed candidates when they are called for the interview. If this is done the interview will be conducted on the basis of a high degree of shared factual knowledge.

The interviewer has more to do before the interview. Because he has cut down the time required to give information he has more time to judge the candidate's suitability. He will have some knowledge about the candidate from his application. He needs to consider this data carefully in relation to the tasks the applicant will have to perform. This should lead him to prepare a list of points which demand further exploration during the discussion. In practice this means making a list of points for discussion with all candidates, and a further supplementary list for each interview based on the data available to the interviewer about a particular applicant. The interviewer will now know exactly what information he needs to ascertain during each interview. The skills discussed in this book will help him with this task.

A prime objective is to encourage the candidate to think about himself in relation to the job. As he will, perforce, have to do most of this thinking aloud he will expose much about himself in the process. Thus lowly structured questions which demand expansive answers are to be preferred to questions designed to elicit a defined piece of information. Thus:

"Would you like to tell me how you set about . . ."

is a better question than:

"Have you had experience of . . .?"

Listening and summarizing are also important skills because they enable the interviewer to pick up cues from the applicant, and to ensure that both of them really understand what the other is saying.

The following is a record of an interview for a post in the technical section of a professional institution. The job demands the ability to act as a secretary to professional committees, to write reports and to undertake background work which will aid the committees. As before, I comment on what happens as the interview proceeds.

Interviewer: Thank you for coming. The object of the exercise is for us both to consider whether you would be suitable for one of our vacancies, and for me to decide whether to call you back for a further interview after I have seen a number of other applicants. I see from your application that you went to ——— University. How did you enjoy it? (*A good, no nonsense start to the interview followed by an open question designed to put the candidate at his ease by allowing him to talk about familiar ground. At the same time the candidate is bound to reveal something about himself in his reply*)

178

Applicant: Quite well. Looking back I'd have chosen another subject. In my last year I was president of my hall of residence

I: Why did you switch to —— ? (He named his profession)

A: I didn't want to make a career in science. I wanted commercial experience. I see myself as a professional —— now.

I: Who taught you in that subject at the University?

A: I can't remember

I: I thought it might be Mr ——

A: No, he was the professor

(At this point the Interviewer asked some technical questions which were answered satisfactorily. This was necessary because it seemed strange that a young candidate couldn't remember the name of the person who was his tutor only five years before. This could have been an attack of nerves.)

I: Why did you join —— (*name of a company*) after leaving University?

A: It could have been any firm, but I knew someone who worked there. (*Here the interviewer said nothing and the Applicant continued*) I wanted to join a large firm

I: (*After a pause to allow the applicant to expand on his answer, which he failed to do.*) Did you feel lost in a large company?

A: Yes, it all seemed very impersonal at first but I've stayed there and in a way it's a wrench to leave

I: Would you advise other young people to join a large company?

A: Yes. One problem is that you find yourself involved in only a limited type of work. I've developed some ideas on training students in large companies (*he expanded on this without prompting*).

I: Did you apply to join more than one company when you left University?

A: Three firms ——— turned me down I regret to say. I only got an ordinary degree, but ——— University is tough and I chose the wrong subject

I: How do you set about carrying out research in your subject?

(*This was part of the man's experience with his employers.*)

A: It involves an appraisal of standard procedures. For example, I talked to ——— (*names of companies*), and I've developed some useful ideas and procedures which we now use

I: Tell me about them

(*Here the applicant described his work and ideas in detail*)

I: I see you act as a secretary to a working party. What are the problems associated with acting in that capacity?

A: The main problem is deciding what is the consensus of opinion and if this makes sense. Committees can go round in circles

I: I see your report to Mr ———. What sort of person is he?

A: Capable . . . He allows one to take initiatives and to work under one's own steam, which I enjoy

I: I notice you say in your application that your experience is relevant to the job we're advertising

A: Yes. Reading your memorandum it would seem that the work is similar to what I'm doing. For example, knowing how to find information, and the importance of building good relationships with people. (*These were both points of substance not covered in the paper sent to the applicant*)

I: Why do you want to join us?

A: That's a difficult question. I see this place as a good stepping off post. I only see myself staying here for about three years to broaden my knowledge. Its so easy to become insular. (*The interviewer never discovered why his question was 'difficult'*

I: You say this is a stepping stone. Where would you want to step?

A: To another firm at a higher level than I am now.

I: You say it's a wrench to leave your present company, so why are you thinking of doing so? (*Here the interviewer is displaying an essential skill, the ability to remember and to use what was said sometime before*)

A: Well I have to look at my career prospects

I: Do they not have an appraisal system?

A: Yes, we're appraised every six months, but I don't know how far I'd progress. All I know is that I'll be in my present job for two years

(*The interviewer might have probed more here. Either the six monthly appraisal system has deficiencies, or the applicant is hiding something about what he's been told.*)

I: You say you'd want to go back to another firm after three years here. A larger or a smaller firm?

A: It would have to be a larger firm. I'm interested in research which small firms can't afford

I: As you see we have four vacancies in the section. Would you put them in rank order of interest to you?

(*The applicant mentioned one and said the others didn't interest him as much.*)

A: Its important that a job should interest one

I: So it's ——— or nothing?

A: Yes
I: What are the rules for being a good chairman of a working party?
A: He should keep firm control and mustn't deter people from speaking —— (*The interviewer said nothing*) —— It is also important that his terms of reference are clear —— (*The interviewer said nothing and then both men started talking at once*)
I: Sorry ——
A: No —— (*What might have been said was lost forever*)
I: What would you do if your chairman transgressed your rules?
A: Try and draw his attention to the terms of reference which he hadn't covered
I: How would you do this diplomatically?
A: It depends on the individual. Certainly I wouldn't do it during a meeting. By way of suggestion. After all you're only a secretary even if you have views
I: Are there any questions you'd like to ask?
A: Could you tell me more about the mix of work I'd be doing?
I: (*The interviewer told him*) You'll be allowed to get on with things on your own. (*He'd remembered that this was important to the candidate.*)
A: How long do people normally stay in this job?
I: It varies. To stay less than two years isn't really fair to either party
A: How much of my work would be controlled by a committee chairman. Would I deal with them?
I: Yes. You'd have a dual responsibility to your chairman and your supervisor
A: Should we discuss conditions of service later?
I: Yes I think so

(*And so the interview came to an end.*)

The reader will have noticed that the majority of the talking during the interview was done by the applicant, yet by asking skilful questions the interviewer kept control of its direction and pace. Further, he remembered what the applicant had said and referred back to previous remarks when framing questions. The skill of summarizing was not used explicitly in this interview. Our man preferred to reflect back remarks made by the applicant, eg 'You say . . .'. Above all this interviewer allowed the candidate the maximum opportunity to display how his skills and previous experience were relevant to the vacancy. In doing this the candidate revealed a great deal about himself.

CHAPTER 13

Some thoughts on management development and the development of managers

Management development has been one of our major growth industries since the end of World War II. In three decades we have moved from a position that 'training' is an act of faith which will pay off at some unspecified time in the future, to the current realization that management development is a highly complex process, involving at one end the examination of group targets and activities and at the other, the interaction of individuals. Along the way we have invented a whole host of fashionable jargon. Organization Development, Management by Objectives, Managerial Grid, T Groups, Transactional Analysis, are now phrases which trip off the tongue of any with-it manager. Behind all this thinking and experimentation lies one solid fact, namely the recognition by chief executives that their managers are one of the most precious resources available to them.

Money, machines, market potential, a good product, are all vital ingredients of any company's prosperity, but none of them can be of value unless it is harnessed and used by people. Of the human resources a company uses its managers (and this term includes all those responsible for the work of others) are the men and women whose initiative, brainpower, leadership and organizing abilities play a vital part in translating inanimate resources and ideas into tangible proof of a company's ability to meet a market need. It need be no surprise, therefore, that chief executives are vitally concerned with management development. Nor is it a surprise that many are eager to embrace the latest fashion or idea, in the hope that at long last someone has thought up a solution which will ensure that in the future their managers will perform in an improved manner.

Many of the ideas which have been developed have been of great value, particularly in those companies whose chief executive has devoted time and thought to what has been attempted. Job descriptions, appraisal schemes, the setting and agreeing of targets of performance in key areas, analysis of organization in relation to expected goals, and some of the work designed to improve inter-personal relationships have all been beneficial, particularly when they have been seen as a means to an end and not an end in themselves. Often the benefits have accrued in terms of a more rational or healthy business and to this extent it may be assumed that managers, as a group, have benefited.

Today we lay increasing emphasis on group working and group performance. There is nothing wrong in this provided that we remember that groups are made up of individuals and that the pursuit of individual excellence (properly harnessed and working harmoniously with others in the group), is a necessary ingredient for the health of any business. The various methods of management development, many beneficial in themselves, do not necessarily result in any given individual being motivated, encouraged or developed to the utmost of his capability. Various ways have been tried to deal with individual improvement. Individual training plans, regular talks with the 'boss', counselling, coaching, and sending a man on a course are some of the familiar methods. Of these perhaps course attendance is one of the most popular. Ask the majority of managers what they understand by training and they respond 'going on a course'. Such is the impact of our schooldays, that we equate formal learning with a classroom!

In my professional work I have discussed the individual training plans of subordinates with many of their managers. Too often the only suggested way of satisfying an identified training need is by sending a man on a course. Seldom does a manager propose to act as a coach to his own subordinate. Coaching is not the answer to all problems of helping a subordinate to gain knowledge and experience, but it is an essential supplement to the more usual methods employed, such as course attendance, guided reading, projects or job rotation. In all these the aim is to improve the performance of the individual manager. An attempt is made to help him to acquire more knowledge or to develop his skills in managing. Possession of certain skills are necessary prerequisites for any successful manager. He must be able to forecast and plan, to organize, to lead and to control. Although these concepts may be learned from books, or on a course, every practising manager knows that a gap exists between theory and practice. This gap does not lessen the need to understand the theory—rather it emphasizes the importance of adapting it to the practical situation in which the manager has to perform. Few management concepts are of value to an individual until they have been proved worthwhile, through trial and error, in the working situation. Because managers are busy men, few of them have the time or the opportunity to test in practice what they have read or learned from a textbook or on a course. Pressure of work, the indifference of his superior, or any other of the many day to day pressures militate against a manager spending time to test a new idea. It is the superior manager who can help to close the gap by demonstrating that he is willing to devote his own precious time to helping and encouraging his subordinate to apply the lessons he has learned on a course, or on a seminar, or through reading.

The utility of courses, particularly those run on conventional lines, can be questioned. Thus in the Mant report:[1]

> The general pattern seems to be that the 'better' experienced managers are sent on external courses, and the rest either receive no management training (usually in smaller firms), or internal 'conditioning' courses in larger firms.
>
> Conditioning courses have the benefit of bringing managers from different functions together, but usually for the purpose of listening to lectures. A typical lecture is devoted to company policy (as received doctrine), rarely to the development or functions of policy (as a management tool). *The trainer's job is thus exposition, not exploration . . .* We formed the impression that much of the information dispensed in in-company training courses might be dealt with by more imaginative company information systems. (Author's italics).

Exposition has its place in helping a manager to acquire new ideas or knowledge, but it is exploration which turns the ideas or knowledge to practical use. The major role of a coach is not to impart knowledge but to help a manager to explore.

In another study of management training and development, initiated by the Central Training Council[2] some assumptions are made about the subject:

Managers can be helped to learn, they are not wholly at the mercy of accidents of birth or situation. Learning is not an end in itself, but is a means of improving performance.

Management training was at an unsatisfactory level in British industry at large . . .

This, again, underlines the gap between learning and action, between the need for a manager to acquire knowledge and the assistance he requires to apply what he has learned. Figure 13.1 shows the analysis of post-course responses by members of 13 courses held at the Urwick Management Centre. They allow a comparison to be made between the stated main subject interests of the managers and their assessment of the utility of the course in each subject area. There are two points to make about these results. First, there is a high correlation (.93) between what was felt to be useful on the course and the managers' own interests. This does no more than demonstrate that any worthwhile course should be preceded by some kind of analysis to ensure that what is being covered corresponds in some way to the needs of those attending.

Secondly, and of much greater importance, is the list of the six subject areas which the managers felt to be of most interest to them. They were:

Finance
Management by objectives
Man management
Network planning
Long range planning
Recruitment and selection.

Bearing these in mind as *post-course* responses (ie responses after attending a six week course and therefore conditioned by the course) look at figure 13.2 which is an analysis of a pre-course questionnaire designed to determine what managers concluded were their most pressing current problems at work. The nine problem areas which headed the list were:

Organization
Communications
Man management
Morale
Recruitment
Personnel
Unions
Training
Lack of policy.

The list of subject areas in figures 13.1 and 13.2 do not correspond because most of the subject areas in Figure 13.2 cannot be dealt with satisfactorily on a course. Insofar as the subject areas in figure 13.1 appear on figure 13.2 (recruitment, technical, accounting) the last two have a relatively low response rate on figure 13.2 but a high response rate on figure 13.1.

We can conclude from this that courses are an inappropriate medium for dealing with many of the day to day problems of managers, but that they can be of use, if carefully structured, in helping managers to acquire knowledge of specialist subject areas. This is borne out by some additional responses from individuals to a questionnaire asking course members to state questions to which they would like the course to provide an answer:

1 What means are available to non-financial managers which will help them to interpret financial information?
2 What systems are currently available to ensure that the best use is made of available technical information?

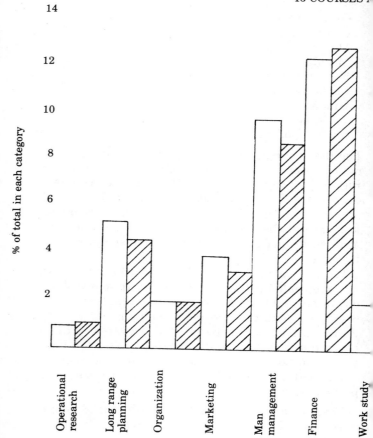

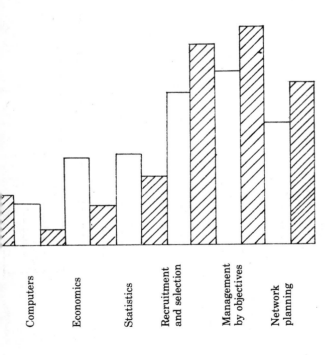

☐ Stated main subject interest

▨ Stated course of practical use
in main interest area

Computers

Economics

Statistics

Recruitment
and selection

Management
by objectives

Network
planning

Figure 13.1

191

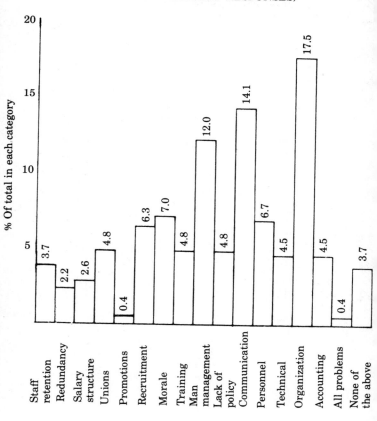

Figure 13.2

ANALYSIS OF CURRENT PROBLEMS BY 13 COURSES

(COURSE MEMBERS' RESPONSES)

3 What factors should be taken into account to ensure objective assessment of personnel in selection or appraisal situations?

4 What means are available to measure the effectiveness of an organization?

5 What means are available to ensure the best recruitment, selection and retention of staff when skilled labour is in short supply?

6 What is the best way to ensure management/worker cooperation?

7 How can we measure job performance of managers and what means are available to advise and to inform managers of how they are doing and how they can improve their performance?

8 What are the merits of various budgetary control systems?

Courses held internally can deal adequately with some of the subject areas listed in Figure 13.2. An internal course does mean, however, that those attending are deprived of the benefit of meeting managers from other organizations. This is a severe loss if the internal course is only a replica of one held at an outside institution. To be of real value an internal course should be structured so that there is genuine free discussion of many of the subject areas listed in Figure 13.2. But such discussion can only be of value if it is centred on an exploration of a problem area, rather than the exposition of a solution which senior management or the trainer thinks to be appropriate. This means coaching as opposed to teaching in the classroom. The case history given later in this chapter illustrates one means of achieving this.

The inference which can reasonably be drawn from this short discussion of some methods currently used to develop management is that all of them, if properly designed and carefully implemented, can be of value in widening a man's knowledge and experience. But to improve a man's performance in his present job demands must be made on his ability. This implies that the tasks he is assigned, and the results expected from his performance, must be of obvious benefit to the organization. Unless the job is a real job the man will not feel challenged—indeed he will spend much of his working day finding activities to pass the time, and in extreme cases such activities may well be detrimental to the company which employs him. At the beginning of the eighteenth century, Isaac Watts wrote in his *Divine Songs for Children*:

> In works of labour, or of skill,
>   I would be busy too,
> For Satan finds some mischief still
>   For idle hands to do.

Substitute 'have worthwhile tasks' for 'be busy' in the second line and, for the loss of metre, we gain a maxim which is appropriate to those whose job it is to assign roles and tasks in organizations.

In a textile company senior management complained constantly about the quality of the supervision. Senior management felt that the supervisory force, although capable in technical matters, were unable to plan the smooth flow of work through the factory and to control costs and deal adequately with the minor crises which are inevitable in any modern factory. Production planning, quality control and cost control systems were available and although, no doubt, each was capable of improvement, they were as good as most systems to be found in the industry at that time. The supervisors had been sent on both external and internal courses, but little improvement resulted. At this stage an organization study was carried out. This showed that there were three levels of supervision—senior supervisors,

supervisors and junior supervisors. The job descriptions for each job were rewritten to assign tasks and areas of responsibility for each man. It became clear that the supervisors had been responsible for part of the work of senior supervisors and part of the work of the junior supervisors. In other words there was a level of supervision too many and this had resulted in wasteful duplication of effort. One of the first results of the reorganization, which created a structure in which there were only senior supervisors and supervisors, was to help each man to understand exactly what role he was expected to play. The results were encouraging both in terms of work output and in individual job satisfaction.

Being given a demanding job implies that a man should understand his role, agree on the tasks for which he is to be responsible and set, in conjunction with his manager, standards of performance which can be used as evidence of attainment. Only in this way can the necessary conditions be present in which a man can identify a challenge, take steps to meet it and have pride in his success. These are prerequisites for success in developing managers. Without them a man is unlikely to recognize the need for improvement, and if this recognition is absent his desire to learn will be seriously impaired. Additional knowledge is of interest, but rarely seems vital to improved performance on the job.

Coaching implies imparting any necessary knowledge, developing skills and changing attitudes. Successful coaching depends on the ability to help a man to think for himself, rather than to supply answers or to do his thinking for him. Other means of manager development can supplement the efforts of a coach, but they can never be an effective substitute for the day to day contact and help which any good 'boss' should provide for his subordinates. To quote Douglas McGregor:[3]

> Every encounter between a superior and subordinate involves learning of some kind for the subordinate. (It should involve learning for the superior too, but that is another matter.) When the boss gives an order, asks for the job to be done, reprimands, praises . . . deals with a mistake . . . or takes any other action with subordinates, he is teaching them something . . .

Motivation*

Managers often ask how men can be inspired to make the effort to tackle a job with enthusiasm and imagination. The short answer is that people cannot be forced to do something they do not wish to do. Some would take the view that a galley slave was motivated to row by the whip, or that economic necessity moves a man to work. But did the galley slave, or the man in fear of the sack, give of their best endeavour? Could they be trusted to perform well if the sanctions against inadequate performance were eased or withdrawn?

In an age when detailed supervision of performance is not possible an approach with more relevance to the problem of motivation must be sought. A starting point is to recognize ways of creating conditions in which a man will wish to work well. Many readers will be familiar with Professor Herzberg's thesis that man has two different sets of needs—maintenance or hygiene needs, and motivational needs such as rec-

*For a full discussion of this important subject the reader is referred to *Motivation and Management Development* by Robert E Tannehill, Butterworths, 1970

196

ognition, responsibility, achievement and growth. The hygiene needs include salaries, physical working conditions, fringe benefits and so on. These are aspects about which a man must be satisfied before he is willing to put himself out to give that extra bit of effort which is every superior manager's dream of a good performance by a subordinate. The motivation needs arise from job structure and management style. If a man feels that his job is interesting and important, if his superior manager overtly trusts him and delegates responsibility, then the climate is right for the man to want to give of his best.

The manager, as a coach, has a primary responsibility for creating the conditions which satisfy Herzberg's motivators. One reason for this is that he should know his subordinates better than others. Some men are more ready than others to accept responsibility; the way in which good performance or effort is recognized should vary in order to appear sincere to each individual. There can be no rules here, only the application of principles adapted to what each manager knows of his own situation and of his subordinates.

Let us examine a few of the principles in more detail. First, the structure of the job and the expected results. This requires more than a conventional job description or even the identification of key result areas. We should be concerned more with the minutiae of tasks which in total add up to the achievement of a key result. For example, if improvement of quality in a section is required, what tasks have to be performed to achieve this? These detailed tasks will develop and change as the situation develops and improvement takes place. Delegation here means more than giving responsibility for an overall area; it implies agreeing with the man that he will have a share of doing the interesting tasks.

Could your subordinate attend a meeting, or visit another site or company, when you would normally go yourself? The essence of delegation is imagination. Job enrichment for a manager need not involve a major reorganization. Often it can be achieved by asking oneself 'Do I really need to do this—or could it be left to my subordinate?'

A manager, when discussing expected results or performance standards with a subordinate, needs to balance the latter's view of what can be achieved with the needs of the organization. Clearly there may be disparity between them. It is of no avail to impose standards which a man feels are impossible to achieve. Locke and Bryan found that a man's statements about how he intended to perform and the goals he expected to achieve were good indicators of his later actual performance. The skilful manager will explore with his man how to reconcile the goals required by the organization and the goals felt to be achievable by the man.

There is an important connection between realistic goal setting and a man's abilities, or at least his own assessment of his abilities. A man who tries hard but lacks knowledge or skill will not achieve results. Here again the skills of the coach come into play. He needs to assess how much preliminary information the man requires and the way in which this knowledge should be acquired. So when agreeing work tasks with his man the senior manager should ask himself "Does this man have the necessary knowledge to be able to achieve the results expected?" This establishes the relationship between goal setting, effort, coaching and training.

The next principle is that adequate control information must be available to the man to enable him to assess his progress towards his goals. The answers to 'How well am I doing?' are a major spur to any extra effort required. Just as the middle or long distance runner requires to know his lap times, so a manager needs knowledge about the interim results he is achieving. Here again the coach requires to ensure that knowledge of results is available either by providing it himself or encouraging the man to set up his own monitoring system.

There is an important distinction between knowledge of results and criticism. Much of the research into performance appraisal has shown not only that criticism makes people defensive, but that it leads often to a worsening of performance rather than to the desired improvement. This is not surprising if one thinks of one's own experience and attitudes when being criticized. Only if we are self-critical are we motivated to improve because of dissatisfaction with our own performance. So the skill of coaching is to help the man to assess his own performance and to be dissatisfied with it, rather than to criticize the subordinate himself, which only leads to argument, or insincere agreement, or some other manifestation of defensiveness.

The key factors for the coach to watch if he aspires to create conditions in which his subordinate will wish to improve are:

- structure the job with him in such a way that he will feel that it is interesting
- agree standards for the tasks which the man understands to be reasonable
- ensure that the man can monitor his own performance
- consider whether he needs any extra input of knowledge to be able to do the job
- don't forget that the hygiene factors must be right.

The first four of these are firmly within the control of most bosses. They demand only thought, time and determination to apply. If these are present then many of the problems of motivation will lessen. Nothing succeeds like success in helping a man to feel interest in and to derive satisfaction from his work. Good managers and coaches consciously attempt to stack the cards so that their subordinates will succeed.

The coaching of groups

Stress has been laid throughout this book on the relationship between a manager and his subordinate. Vital as this is there is also a need to develop teams of people to work together effectively. Much of the work which has been carried out in this field has been termed 'Organization Development'. John Woolhouse[4] defines organization development as:

> a planned attempt, led by senior people in the organization, to change the 'style' and climate in which people work. It is a programme of action, not solely a programme of education, planned over a considerable period of time, and using teams rather than individuals as the 'agents of change'.

There are many aspects of a successful programme for the development of the organization. That which concerns us here utilizes the skills of coaching during group sessions forming an integral part of the wider process. The following is a case history illustrating the use of these skills at the start of one such programme.

> *Molins Ltd employs some 5,000 people. Its major division designs and makes cigarette making machinery and it is a world leader in this field. Indeed until after World War II it held a virtual monopoly, though this is now being seriously*

challenged by three foreign competitors. Although a machine manufacturer Molins is keenly sensitive to changes in the consumer market for cigarettes. New brands, or expansion into new markets by the world's cigarette manufacturers, depend for their success on a close relationship between market research, marketing strategy, and production capacity. The last is planned for specific deadline dates and the machine manufacturer is expected to deliver his machines on time. This might not be difficult if the product were mass produced. In Molins' case, however, not only are the machines designed for individual customers, but they incorporate modifications in design, geared to last minute market requirements, during the course of manufacture. Basically the company is faced with the problem of producing small batches of a highly complex machine to a tight delivery schedule in circumstances which make mass production impossible. The majority of employees are time served craftsmen, supervised and managed by men who, in most cases, have spent a lifetime in the service of the firm. There is no lack of job interest: every day presents a new crop of challenges to be overcome. During the last decade the expansion of the business, and the need to meet the challenge of competition, have added the additional problems of production planning, cost control and labour relations to the over-riding need to produce a complex piece of machinery of high quality on time. It says much for the management and employees that maintenance of the quality of product is not *one of the problems which causes concern.*

However, other problems have appeared, mainly among the supervisory group. The increasing size of the company has made lateral communication between its various component departments and sections more difficult. The necessary introduction of specialist departments, such as production planning, cost control and personnel has appeared to supervisors to lessen their authority. Increases in the size and changes in the composition of the labour force have changed the relationship between the supervisor and his team. A situation has arisen when the specialist departments or the unions were blamed for production pressures which arose mainly from changes in world-wide market demand. Clearly recognizing what was happening top management took action. Supervisors were encouraged to attend outside courses to increase their knowledge and understanding of modern management processes. Valuable as these were they made little impact on the basic problems. In this situation what was needed was that groups of supervisors and middle managers should discuss a well recognized work problem, and isolate actions which could be taken individually or collectively to improve the position. Top management selected the problem of delivering on time as the core problem for discussion. A series of weekend meetings for 20 people took place at an hotel. Each participant received a letter from the managing director and another from his site general manager, inviting him to attend and explaining the purpose of the meeting. There was no published time-table because the aim was to enable the participants to discuss what they felt to be important, rather than to impose the detailed subject matter on them. It was agreed that there would be no lectures.

After dinner on the first evening the company sales director talked briefly on 'Our customer's view of our delivery problem'. This key-note talk set the scene and underlined the relevance of the subject. Following this the participants formed three *groups, each group composed of men from different sections of the manufacturing side of the business. The groups were asked to note down those items which in their view contributed to the problem of delivering on time. The following morning these lists were displayed. The three groups produced 22 items between them and these are shown as figure 13.3. At this stage the consultant explained what it was hoped to achieve. He stressed that none of the problems could be solved at the session, nor that agreement on what action should be taken was likely. He suggested that it would be possible to:*

define areas for further action and investigation
understand more precisely the real nature of some of the problems revealed
help individuals to 'commit themselves more positively to helping to solve the problems'. 'Everyone can play a part—no problem is the sole responsibility of a specialist department.'

Finally, he defined his role as helping the participants to define their attitudes and expectations. The consultant could help to bring out inconsistencies in thinking, but he could not suggest solutions; this was their job.

The remainder of the day was spent by the participants either working in syndicates or as a group in order to examine the job of line management in relation to the problems of delivery. Line management tasks could be made more or less difficult by the nature of the support given by specialist departments. Some of the problems arising from the interrelationship of specialists and line managers were discussed in detail. For example, one of the causes of late delivery was stated to be the inadequacy of the bonus scheme. Some managers wished this to be replaced by a more sophisticated arrangement

Figure 13.3
Things contributing to not producing on time

1 All round lack of enthusiasm for job
2 Bad industrial relations
3 Trade union activity leading to erosion of effort
4 Too many breakdowns: machine tools not reliable
5 Fixed lead times unrealistic
6 Bonus system abused and can't be used for estimating
7 Supervisors lack power
8 Lack of liaison between departments
9 Stock holding of common parts too low
10 Demarcation problems between assemblers and testers
11 Lookout and assembly documents don't coincide
12 All modifications not necessary
13 Insufficient tooling available
14 Pre-production planning inadequate
15 Programme constantly changing
16 Shortage of skilled labour (don't utilize fully what we have)
17 Lack of labour discipline
18 Wage structure and hours of work not common
19 Production time for new type of machine inadequate
20 Lack of production knowledge in design department
21 Capacity of machines between shops not balanced
22 Variable parts decided too late

based on work study standards. The group first examined what criteria an ideal bonus scheme should satisfy to be fair to both management and the workforce. The Molins scheme was then examined against these criteria. Although it fell short of the ideal there was general agreement that if certain changes were made in the administration of the scheme it would meet most of the company's present needs. Additionally certain aspects of the scheme which required further examination were emphasized. The major lesson of this discussion for the participants was that line supervisors and managers could do much within the framework of the current scheme to overcome some of their problems.

After dinner the group was joined by the managing, production and personnel directors and by the site general manager. The group discussed with them in detail four items from the list shown as figure 13.3. As a result of the discussion certain lines of action were agreed upon and these later became the responsibility of a senior manager.

The following are some of the main points illustrated by this case history:

1 The discussion centred on a work problem which all the participants felt to be important.
2 There were no lectures. The group discussed aspects of the problem with inputs as required from the tutor or specialist manager.
3 The tutor used the coaching skills of listening, questioning, discussing and summarizing to help the group to formulate its ideas.
4 Top management showed that they thought the exercise was important by their own participation late at night.
5 A programme of the follow-up action required was worked out and implemented.

The session in itself did nothing more than establish a suitable base for follow-up action. This was achieved not by lecturing or exhorting the group, but rather by encouraging them to discover their problems for themselves, suggesting outline plans for solutions and testing these on top management. The learning process was integrated with commitment to action. This is a sound method of developing managers. It involved them as a group. Reliance on a course alone often fails to change work behaviour.

Coaching is a participatory exercise. It is no substitute for leadership but it does enable a leader to achieve one of his aims namely the development of his subordinates' capacity to exercise intelligently the skills and knowledge which they possess. The following quotation from a leader in *The Times* of 18 October 1971 sums up the thesis of this book:

> A million managers every day have an opportunity to help their subordinates to develop essential skills—in situations far more realistic and important than management courses, seminars, and so on. The manager rarely sees himself as a coach yet every time he discusses a problem with a junior colleague and asks the question: 'What do you think?' he is unwittingly encouraging for good or bad the development of his colleagues' managerial skills. The opportunity should not be wasted.

1 MANT A, *The Experienced Manager,* BIM 1969.
2 Survey on Management Training and Development, Department of Employment, 1971.
3 McGREGOR D, *The Human Side of Enterprise*, McGraw Hill, 1960.
4 TORRINGTON D P and SUTTON D F, eds, *Handbook of Management Development*, Gower Press, 1973.

BIBLIOGRAPHY

Chapter 1

EMPLOYMENT, Department of, *Survey on management training and development*. London, HMSO, 1971. 70 pp

MCGREGOR, DOUGLAS, *Human side of enterprise*. New York, McGraw-Hill, 1960. 246 pp

STEWART, ROSEMARY, *Managers and their jobs*. A study of the similarities and differences in the ways managers spend their time. London, Macmillan, 1967. 186 pp

Chapter 2

FOOD, DRINK AND TOBACCO INDUSTRY TRAINING BOARD, *Development at work: a practical handbook for managers*. Gloucester, The Training Board, 1978. 2 vols.

HUMBLE, JOHN *Editor*, *Improving the performance of the experienced manager*. Maidenhead, Berkshire, McGraw-Hill, 1973. 346 pp. Bibliog in text

SIDNEY, ELIZABETH *and others*, *Skills with people: a guide for managers*. London, Hutchinson, 1973. 232 pp. Bibliog in text

Chapter 3

CRIBBIN, JAMES J, *Effective managerial leadership*. New York, American Management Association, 1972. 264 pp.

Chapter 4

DRAKE, RICHARD I *and* SMITH, PETER J, *Behavioural science in industry*. Maidenhead, Berkshire, McGraw-Hill, 1973. 134 pp. Bibliog in text

GELLERMAN, SAUL W, *Behavioral science in management*. Harmondsworth, Middlesex, Penguin Books, 1974. 133 pp

INSTITUTE OF PERSONNEL MANAGEMENT, *The behavioural sciences: techniques of application* by Patrick Sills. London, The Institute, 1973. 48 pp

NATIONAL INDUSTRIAL CONFERENCE BOARD, *Behavioral science: concepts and management application*. New York, The Board, 1969. 178 pp. (Personnel Policy Study no. 216). Bibliog

Chapter 5

ADAIR, JOHN, *Training for communication.* Farnborough, Hants, Gower Press, Teakfield Ltd., 1973. 205 pp. Bibliog

BORGER, R and SEABORNE, A E M, *The psychology of learning.* Harmondsworth, Middlesex, Penguin Books, 1966. 243 pp. Bibliog

BUZAN, TONY, *Use your head.* London, British Broadcasting Corporation, 1974. 144 pp. Bibliog

DAVIES, IVOR K, *The management of learning.* Maidenhead, Berkshire, McGraw-Hill, 1971. 256 pp. Bibliog in text

EMPLOYMENT AND PRODUCTIVITY, Department of, *The discovery method in training* by Dr R M Belbin. London, HMSO, 1969. 43 pp. (Training Information Paper no. 5)

HONEY, PETER, *Face to face:* a practical guide to interactive skills. London, Institute of Personnel Management, 1976. 149 pp.

Chapter 6

HOLROYDE, GEOFFREY, *How to delegate:* a practical guide. Rugby, Mantec Publications, 1970. 34 pp

THE INDUSTRIAL SOCIETY, Delegation by Andrew Forrest. London, The Society, July 1972. 24 pp. (Notes for Managers no. 19)

LAIRD, DONALD A *and* LAIRD, ELEANOR C, *The techniques of delegating:* how to get things done through others. New York, McGraw-Hill, 1957. 195 pp. Bibilog

Chapters 7 and 8

ADAIR, JOHN, *Training for decisions.* Farnborough, Hants, Gower Press, Teakfield Ltd, 1971. 167 pp. Bibliog

AMERICAN MANAGEMENT ASSOCIATION, *Coaching, learning and action* by Bill C Lovin and Emery Reber Casstevens. New York, AMA, 1971. 169 pp. Bibliog

CONSTRUCTION INDUSTRY TRAINING BOARD, A guide to coaching for management. London, *The Board*, 1974. 12 pp

KEPNER, CHARLES H *and* TREGOE, BENJAMIN B, *The rational manager:* a systematic approach to problem solving and decision making. 2nd ed. New Jersey, Princeton, Kepner-Tregoe Inc, 1976. 263 pp. Bibliog

STROHMER, ARTHUR F, *The skills of managing.* Reading, Massachusetts, Addison-Wesley, 1970. 149 pp

Chapter 10

ANSTEY, EDGAR *and others, Staff appraisal and development*

208

London, Allen & Unwin, 1976. 242 pp. Bibliog

ASHRIDGE MANAGEMENT COLLEGE, *The design of appraisal systems* by W A G Braddick and P J Smith. Berkhampstead, Ashridge Management College, nd 27 pp

BEVERIDGE, W E, *the interview in staff appraisal*. London, Allen & Unwin, 1975. 132 pp. Bibliog

INDUSTRIAL SOCIETY, *Appraisal and appraisal interviewing* by Brian Scott and Barry Edward. London, The Society, 1972. 39 pp. (Notes for Managers no. 18)

INSTITUTE OF PERSONNEL MANAGEMENT, *Staff appraisal* by Dr G A Randell, P M A Packard, R L Shaw and A J Slater. rev ed. London, The Institute, 1974. 152 pp. Bibliog

MAIER, NORMAN R F, *The appraisal interview:* three basic approaches. La Jolla, California, University Associates, 1976. 228 pp. Bibliog

Chapter 12

BRITISH INSTITUTE OF MANAGEMENT FOUNDATION, *How to interview* by D Mackenzie Davey and P McDonnell. London, British Institute of Management Foundation, 1975. 51 pp. Bibliog

FRASER, JOHN M, *Employment interviewing*. 5th ed. London, MacDonald & Evans, 1978. 217 pp

NATIONAL INSTITUTE OF INDUSTRIAL PSYCHOLOGY, *The seven point plan* by Alec Rodger, 1972. 19 pp. (NIIP Paper no. 1). Bibliog

SHOUKSMITH, GEORGE, *Assessment through interviewing*. 2nd ed. Oxford, Pergamon Press, 1978. 149 pp

Chapter 13

COTTON AND ALLIED TEXTILES INDUSTRY TRAINING BOARD, Developing effective management: a guide to the training and development of existing and future managers, supervisors, with particular reference to the changing environment in which they work. Manchester, The Board, May 1975. 4 brochures

INSTITUTE OF PERSONNEL MANAGEMENT, *Developing effective managers* by Tom Roberts. rev ed. 1974. 168 pp. Bibliog

Developing resourceful managers by John Morris and John G Burgoyne. IPM, 1973. 86 pp. Bibliog

PEDLER, MIKE *and others*, *A manager's guide to self-development*. Maidenhead, Berkshire, McGraw-Hill, 1978. 231 pp. Bibliog in text

INDEX